Praise for ADHD in Teens & Young Adults

"*ADHD in Teens and Young Adults* is a rich and useful resource that will provide helpful, practical tools not just for adolescents with ADHD, but for all adolescents. Guided by experience and research, Melissa Springstead Cahill breaks down skills into easy to implement steps, and empowers her readers with powerful strategies and approaches that can change minds and brains."

—**Tina Payne Bryson, PhD, LCSW**, co-author of the *New York Times* bestselling books *The Whole-Brain Child* and *No-Drama Discipline*, Executive Director of The Center for Connection and The Play Strong Institute

"Teens and young adults who work through the eight step ANCHORED approach presented in this wonderful book will breathe a sigh of relief as they become better organized, more focused and able to get things done on time while feeling less stressed and more confident. Every teen or young adult with ADHD and anyone who helps them needs this book."

—**Debra Burdick, LCSW**, author of *Mindfulness Skills Workbook for Kids and Teens* and *Mindfulness for Teens with ADHD*

"Many, many teens struggle with self-organization and staying on track with home, school and extracurricular responsibilities. Any kid (whether formally diagnosed with ADHD or not) will benefit a great deal from Dr. Melissa Springstead Cahill's exciting new book. It's chock full of straightforward mindfulness-based skill practices, along with very helpful worksheets and planner tools that make getting organized and effective in managing the everyday routines of teen-dom much more do-able. Melissa's book should find itself tucked (neatly!) into every less-than-ideally organized kiddos' backpack!"

—**Mitch Abblett, PhD**, author of *The Challenging Child Toolbox, Growing Mindful Card Deck*, and *The Five Hurdles to Happiness*

D1608304

ADHD iN TeENs & YoUNG AdULtS

A Mindfulness Workbook to Keep You ANCHORED

Melissa Springstead Cahill, PsyD

ADHD In Teens and Young Adults copyright © 2019 by Melissa Springstead Cahill

Published by:
PESI Publishing & Media
PESI, Inc.
3839 White Ave.
Eau Claire, WI 54703

Cover Design: Amy Rubenzer
Editing: Jenessa Jackson, PhD
Layout: Amy Rubenzer & Bookmasters

Printed in the United States of America
ISBN: 9781683732075
All rights reserved.

PESI
Publishing
& Media
www.publishing.pesi.com

About the Author

Dr. Melissa Springstead Cahill, PsyD is the owner and executive director of Anchor Children and Family Counseling in Pasadena, California. For the last 12 years, she has dedicated her career to the psychosocial and mental health needs of adolescents. She specializes in working with those who struggle with ADHD, learning disabilities, and other educational barriers.

Dr. Cahill received her master's degree in Marriage and Family Therapy from the University of Southern California and her doctorate in Psychology from the Chicago School of Professional Psychology. When she is not working directly with her clients, Dr. Cahill can often be found at one of Anchor's several events, where she presents on a variety of mental health and wellness topics to schools, non-profits, and numerous professional organizations throughout the Greater Los Angeles Area.

Dedication

This book is dedicated to anyone out there who is struggling in school and scared about the future. With some hard work and dedication, you can and will achieve whatever you put your mind to. Keep your head forward, your heart open, and follow your dreams!

Table of Contents

An Introduction for Clinicians, Psychologists, and Healthcare Workers

A BRIEF OVERVIEW OF ADHD

Attention-deficit/hyperactivity disorder (ADHD) is one of the most fascinating, and undoubtedly one of the most prevalent, psychological disorders. While it remains a relatively new category as far as mental health diagnoses are concerned, its symptoms have been well-documented since the nineteenth century. Thus, most clinicians and support staff currently working in the mental health field are familiar with its most common symptom presentations, including inattention, hyperactivity, and impulsivity. As increased awareness has been brought to the disorder, the number of diagnoses has skyrocketed. In 1996, the National Institute of Mental Health estimated that 4.1% of American children between the ages of nine and 17 were affected by ADHD (Strock, 2006), whereas this figure climbed to one in 20 by 2003 (Faraone et al., 2003). Other estimates suggest that the prevalence rate may be as high as one out of every 11 school-age children in the United States (Pastor et al., 2015).

Today, ADHD is considered to be a chronic disorder caused by a combination of neurobiological and genetic factors. However, in my clinical practice I have found that, among the general population, many think of ADHD as a "non-serious" psychological condition, especially in comparison to more severe brain disorders (such as, but not limited to, Parkinson's, Epilepsy, or Schizophrenia). However, this perspective misrepresents ADHD's ability to affect several dimensions of a person's life. Children and adolescents who experience symptoms of ADHD often have trouble staying focused, have difficulty sitting still, encounter problems related to acting without thinking, and demonstrate pronounced difficulties in finishing tasks. Each of these traits, especially in a school environment, can erode learning outcomes and result in achievement gaps in comparison to other peers. When left untreated, the disorder can also generate negative long-term effects that include (but are not limited to) an inability to make friends, school failure, and drug abuse—all of which can lead to the development of more severe emotional and psychological problems. Indeed, studies show that 65% of adolescents with ADHD also have one or more comorbid psychiatric conditions that affect multiple areas of their lives (Bierdman, Newcorn, & Sprich, 1991; Zylowska et al., 2008), including mood and anxiety disorders, learning disabilities, disruptive behavior disorders, tics, and Tourette's syndrome (MTA Cooperative Group, 1999). It is thus not surprising that individuals with ADHD often experience additional relational, emotional, developmental, and physical difficulties. Furthermore, as it is a chronic illness, ADHD isn't a diagnosis that children will simply "outgrow" as they enter adulthood. Left untreated, the symptoms and comorbid disorders associated with ADHD often become more numerous and intensify over time.

It is also vital to understand that a person's diagnosis of ADHD doesn't simply affect him or her; rather, it has a ripple effect that extends outwards and through that person's social spheres. At its most severe, symptoms of ADHD can lead to teenage pregnancy, substance abuse, and traffic violations or accidents (Harpin, 2005). Therefore, beyond the direct costs of treating the disorder at a purely medical level, one must also consider the various financial and legal ramifications associated with the disorder (Leibson et al., 2001). Tragically, and for these reasons, ADHD will too often lead to marital and family disturbances as the consequences of the disorder intensify (Harpin, 2005). Furthermore, as individuals with ADHD begin to see the effects of their disorder on the lives of their family, friends, colleagues, fellow students, and/or co-workers, it is common for them to withdraw from social activities due to a distorted sense of self. In other cases, aggressive and oppositional behaviors may develop (Harpin, 2005).

The key takeaway is this: The potential ramifications of ADHD are too great to ignore when it comes to a person's emotional, physical, mental, and financial health. Great care needs to be taken in order to ensure that treatment for the disorder is successful and that all comorbid conditions are adequately addressed. Effective treatment takes not only a patient or client's present status into account, but their future trajectory as well. It almost always needs to include compassion and consideration for the many other stakeholders who are rooting for the success of that individual.

THE LINK BETWEEN ADHD AND EXECUTIVE FUNCTIONING

Simply put, the clinical picture of ADHD has evolved in the last few decades. While the ADHD sufferer was often stereotyped in past years as a restless, impulsive, and hyperactive child, mental health care providers now have a more nuanced understanding of the disorder and whom it affects. ADHD goes beyond issues of focus and restlessness. It affects a person's ability to get started on a task, sustain effort through the task's completion, and regulate any emotions that could disrupt their ability to handle the variety of daily activities that must be completed as part of a normal, balanced life (Brown, 2013). While it is only human to have an *occasional* lapse of memory, to have a hard time finding motivation, or to lose one's cool in the face of strong emotions, people with ADHD often experience *chronic* impairments in these areas.

What each of these elements of ADHD has in common is that they collectively fall under the umbrella of what scientists term "executive functioning"—which refers to the higher-order cognitive processes responsible for prioritizing, integrating, and regulating other cognitive functions (Brown, 2013). The executive functions help us to problem solve, organize tasks, pay attention, make decisions, manage time, exhibit self-restraint, and use our working memory. Individuals with ADHD have deficits in executive functioning, which explains why they exhibit such pronounced difficulties in these areas.

Given the breadth of its definition, executive functioning can at first seem like something of a monolithic concept. As such, scientists have attempted to subdivide the term into smaller, more distinct categories. Barkley's (2012) model of executive functioning is perhaps the most well-known and widely used. From his vantage point, executive functioning is broken down into four main areas: (1) non-verbal working memory, (2) verbal working memory, (3) self-regulation of affect/motivation/arousal, and (4) planning/generativity. At the heart of Barkley's model is an awareness that the executive functioning impairments associated with ADHD often affect an individual's ability to regulate themselves across a variety of domains.

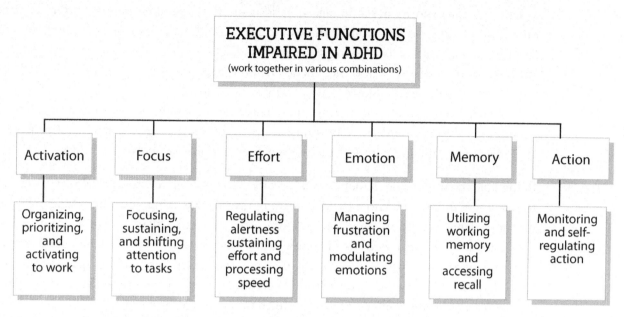

Based on Brown's (2013) Model of ADHD and Executive Functioning Impairment

In contrast to Barkley's model is that of Brown (2005, 2013), who proposed a model consisting of the following six clusters. First is **activation**, or the ability to organize, prioritize, and initiate tasks. Second is **focus**, which Brown describes as successfully bringing one's attention to the task at hand. Third is **effort**, or the ability to sustain purposeful activity on a chosen task, as well as the ability to successfully regulate one's level of alertness to competing stimuli. Fourth is **emotion**, which we can understand as the capacity to regulate strong feelings and manage frustration levels. Fifth is **memory**, including both making use of working memory and being able to recall past information. Sixth and finally is **action**, which Brown describes as the ability to monitor and self-regulate behavior. The strength of this framework is that all six of these clusters are connected, and deficits in any one area will likely lead to deficits as a whole, resulting in a diagnosis of ADHD.

THE UNIQUE CHALLENGE FOR ADOLESCENTS

Clinicians often have difficulty accurately diagnosing ADHD early in childhood, as it is usually age-appropriate for young children to exhibit an inability to sustain attention, follow directions, or accurately complete a series of instructions. Furthermore, these expectations may be downright *impossible* if a child has not yet reached these stages of cognitive development. On the other end of the age spectrum are adults—whether they have been diagnosed with ADHD at one point in their lives or are among the millions of undiagnosed Americans with ADHD—who can seek out a profession of their choosing that is tailored around their relative strengths and weaknesses. For example, an adult with ADHD may choose a vocation where they are outdoors and on their feet rather than one where they must sit behind a desk and sustain focus for extended periods of time. In this respect, adults can have the luxury of knowing that (at least in part) they have control over what they do during the day.

In contrast, the majority of school-age adolescents in the U.S. have their daily routine planned out ahead of time—often months in advance. In school, teachers expect students to sustain attention equally across five or more different subjects (which they may or may not have an aptitude for or interest in), and they make no allowances for fluctuations in attention levels at different times of the day. Simultaneously, there exists a collective expectation among parents and teachers that—in this zone somewhere between childhood and adulthood—adolescents should be taking more initiative in terms of being able to manage their time, effectively plan for long-term goals, and comport themselves as young professionals.

Being able to fulfill these demands is a big task for *any* adolescent, especially at a time when teenagers are inundated with a steady stream of distractions ranging from text messages, social media updates, television shows, new music, and extracurricular demands—and when the very chemistry of their body is changing. Adolescence is also a time when most teenagers are struggling with a psychosocial crisis that pits their need for stability against the need to find their own identity (Erikson, 1980). Therefore, if there's ever a time that a human being's executive functioning will be tested, it is during the teenage years.

Although these challenges can be demanding for any adolescent, it can be downright overwhelming for those with ADHD. It is helpful to visualize the junior high to high school years as a time when a person's executive functioning skills are pushed to the redline. As academic environments become more competitive, as children grow up faster due to a constant mass media inundation, and as social networks make the drama of teenage life only a few taps away, the adolescent with ADHD often flounders when he or she lacks adequate support.

WORKING TOWARD SUCCESSFUL INTERVENTIONS AND SOLUTIONS

The good news is that treatment for ADHD is present and effective—a byproduct, no doubt, of decades of heightened research and numerous pharmacological breakthroughs. Currently, a combination of behavior therapy and medication is found to be the most effective treatment for ADHD. That said, it is important to be aware of our limitations as healthcare providers. Medication and behavioral interventions help with short-term symptom reduction, but their efficacy in the long-term is unclear. An additional complication is that some adolescents do not respond to certain medications, and some experience unbearable side effects. In short, there is no "one size fits all" intervention when it comes to alleviating ADHD symptoms and improving functioning. For this reason, the American Academy of Pediatrics emphasizes the importance of clinicians and families working together to determine whether treatment is effective and, if not, exploring alternatives (Reiff & Tippins, 2003).

THE ANCHORED METHOD

The **ANCHORED** method described in this book is one such alternative that may be used with teenagers and young adults as a supplement to current evidence-based ADHD treatments. This method was born out of a need to develop a program that more fully addressed the social and emotional needs of adolescents with ADHD. When I began formulating this method, it was critical that a core aspect of the approach involved addressing and improving adolescent executive functioning. I began by asking those affected by ADHD—including not only adolescents diagnosed with the disorder, but their parents, educators, and healthcare professionals as well—what they felt was required and/or missing from the way we treat the disorder. The results of that primary research eventually illuminated the pathway to my own dissertation and, in turn, produced the method I am proud to share with you over the pages to come.

One of my goals in crafting ANCHORED was to provide adolescents with the tools they need in order to address any ADHD-related difficulties they encounter throughout their lifespan. **ANCHORED focuses on highlighting ways a young person can become more focused, functional, and happy while living with ADHD.** Mindfulness practices are used throughout ANCHORED, as they have been found to improve attention, memory, emotion regulation, interpersonal relationships, and the ability to cope with stress. Chapter 1 outlines the ANCHORED approach for teens.

HOW TO USE THIS BOOK

The ANCHORED approach consists of eight structured components that should be completed in sequence. Underpinning the whole of this work is a sensitivity to the way that adolescent brains develop. By this, I mean that executive function skills are often still a "work in progress" for most teenagers, especially those with ADHD, and are taught most effectively one step at a time. Therefore, each component is meant to take one week to complete, allowing ample time for the adolescent to practice these newly learned strategies and make them more habitual. I should also mention that the strategies in this book are by no means exclusive to adolescents with ADHD. In fact, the ANCHORED approach is extremely effective for any adolescent wishing to become more grounded, organized, or attuned to their own emotions.

While this preface is written with adults in mind—including parents, educators, mindfulness coaches, and mental health professionals—the remainder of the text speaks directly to the adolescent. ANCHORED normalizes their experiences and emotions. Each week, the text and activities build the adolescent's confidence and competency in navigating their diagnosis.

Any mental health professional working in this field knows what mom and dad already know: that children are special and defined by far more than the sum of their diagnoses or the "healthiness" of their brain. Above all else, the ANCHORED approach finds the dignity and beauty of youth while, at the same time, acknowledging the very real struggles that come with growing up while simultaneously managing a psychological disorder. I very much hope that this book will help you provide another level of support to a child, patient, or client who is dear to you.

An Overview of This Book, and What is ADHD, Anyway?

If you are reading this book, the odds are very likely that you have ADHD.

Your diagnosis might be recent, or it might be something that you have struggled with for several years. For many teens and adolescents in exactly your position, this often feels isolating—like you're the only person in the world with a mysterious set of problems you're trying to make sense of. Above all else, know that you are not alone and that you will be able to learn a set of skills through this book that will help you become healthier and happier across so many different aspects of your life.

It might surprise you to know that ADHD is one of the most common psychiatric disorders in the United States. Currently, doctors think that ADHD is caused by a combination of neurobiological and genetic factors. No two presentations of ADHD are ever 100% alike, but some of the most common symptoms include trouble staying focused, difficulty sitting still, acting without thinking, and difficulty finishing tasks. More specifically, the big book used by psychologists and therapists, like myself—called *The Diagnostic and Statistical Manual of Mental Disorders* (American Psychiatric Association, 2013)—defines ADHD as impairments in inattention, disorganization, hyperactivity, or impulsiveness. ADHD isn't a diagnosis that people outgrow: It's a chronic condition, which means that even though ADHD is most commonly diagnosed in children and adolescents, it's something that remains a part of one's adult life.

While ADHD is commonly diagnosed in younger children, the disorder often presents increasing challenges during the time period between junior high school and a person's 20s. This is usually because social expectations change for people around this age. Teachers and parents/caregivers believe that teenagers and young adults should have less "hand holding" during this time. That is, there's a widespread social belief that adolescents need to become more independent with regard to planning and organizing as they get older. Throughout this book, we refer to this ability to plan and organize as **executive functioning**. While adults may hold this expectation, the reality is that the adolescent brain might simply not be developed in those areas yet, and ADHD in particular is known to disrupt executive functioning.

There's good news and bad news when it comes to ADHD. The bad news is that if ADHD is ignored or untreated, it can lead to long-term consequences, such as difficulty making friends, hardship in school, and a greater desire to turn to drugs or alcohol to solve problems—all of which can lead to the development of more severe emotional problems later down the road.

ADHD can also lead to a variety of what we call "comorbid" psychological conditions, which refers to conditions that happen at the same time. For example, it's not uncommon for the teens (and adults) with whom I work to also be dealing with issues related to depression or anxiety, as well as oppositional behavior or other learning disabilities that sometimes occur side-by-side. ADHD is a real psychological disorder. It is not some "made-up" illness that's "all in your head." I know firsthand how it can affect how you interact with your family, friends, teachers, and neighbors. I know firsthand how negatively it can make people feel about themselves, deep down. I know this because, just like you, I have ADHD as well.

The good news is that there is treatment for those suffering from ADHD, and studies show that it is both useful and effective. Effective treatments make sure to address all areas of your life that affect your day-to-day functioning. This good news is why you're here, right now, reading this book!

HOW THIS BOOK WORKS

The ANCHORED method described in this book helps to address ADHD-related difficulties by teaching skills that can be used throughout your lifespan. By the end of this book, you're going to have learned some valuable tools that will help with both your executive functioning and emotional needs as a person with ADHD.

Each one of the interventions used in the ANCHORED approach is designed to help you improve your quality of life. Whether it's an academic intervention or a breathing exercise, you will learn ways to become more focused, functional, and happy while living with ADHD. You'll also notice that what I call **mindfulness practices** are also used throughout ANCHORED, as they have been found to improve attention, memory, emotion regulation, interpersonal relationships, and the ability to cope with stress.

The ANCHORED approach consists of eight different steps that are presented in a structured order. It incorporates strategies that have been shown to help people with ADHD lead healthier and happier lives. I have relied on the most current scientific research about ADHD and what works in treating it in order to create this book for you. I have confidence that it will work for you because my colleagues and I have seen it work for many other teens and adolescents.

Anything with eight steps and over 100 pages can seem overwhelming at first. Don't let it stress you out! At the beginning of each chapter is a preview box of what is to come — the skills, worksheets and exercises that are included. Each component is meant to take one or more weeks to complete, which will allow you more than enough time to practice each strategy—no matter how busy your life might be. By taking the time to practice these skills and *deliberately* moving at a slower pace, many people find that these intervention strategies eventually become more routine—just like any other habit.

I'm glad you're here, and I am *very* excited to be able to help you!

ChAPtER 1   A: Attention and Acceptance

> **LEARN IT!**
> - A Recap of ADHD: You Are Not Alone!
> - Overview and Description/Format of the ANCHORED Approach
> - ADHD and Executive Functioning
>
> **USE IT!**
> - Time Management and Organization Exercise: *How Full is Your Plate?*
> - Intentions vs. Goal Setting
> - *Mindfulness Introduction and Deep Breathing Exercise*
>
> **ANCHOR IT!**
> - *Mindfulness Meditation Tracking Sheet*

YOU ARE NOT ALONE!

In the forward to this book, we looked at what ADHD was all about. Together, we learned that ADHD is a real psychological disorder that has profound effects on the lives of the children, teens, and adults who deal with its symptoms each day. We also learned that we aren't alone. How many of us are there dealing with ADHD? Well, recent figures suggest it might be as high as 6.1% of the entire population here in the United States—and maybe more, since so many adults are undiagnosed.

How many people is that? Imagine a low estimate of 19.5 *million* people, all struggling with a common disorder. That's more than all the people in Los Angeles, New York City, and Chicago put together. If we all lived side-by-side, it would *easily* be the largest city in the nation. In fact, it would be bigger than all but five states in the United States. You and I are most definitely not the only two people in the world dealing with the symptoms of ADHD.

While each one of us is different, you've also learned a little bit about some of the commonalities of ADHD, including that we have difficulties with executive functioning that can lead to impulsiveness, hyperactivity, difficulty regulating emotions, difficulty maintaining relationships, and hardship with school activities and academic success. We have also learned the importance of treating ADHD and being proactive about obtaining treatment in order to ensure that our lives are as healthy and happy as possible.

With that in mind, let's look a little more closely at the approach you'll be using for the remainder of this book.

WHAT IS THE ANCHORED APPROACH?

ANCHORED is an acronym that represents eight components that help support adolescents and young adults (that is, individuals between 13 and 22 years of age) with ADHD. An anchor symbolizes hope, strength, and stability—all things that this workbook hopes to bring to you as you make the conscious decision to progress through the curriculum. Here is a description of each chapter:

- Chapter 1 is about **Attention and Acceptance.** That is, attention to understanding what ADHD is and learning what this workbook is all about. It also involves accepting that you *can* utilize strategies to help with the symptoms of ADHD.

- Chapter 2 is about **Natural Awareness.** This chapter is an overview of what mindfulness is and how it can help with ADHD. It also includes mindfulness exercises that help develop sensitivity to what is happening in your space, mind, and body, as well as with your time.

- Chapter 3 is about **Concentrating on Purpose.** This chapter acknowledges that concentrating is often difficult and introduces mindfulness exercises to help increase your ability to do so. It also introduces a tool that makes managing homework easier.

- Chapter 4 is about **Happy Homework.** It offers more insight into the stress behind homework and how to tackle school in both the short and long term. It also places importance on maintaining a positive mindset when under stress.

- Chapter 5 is about being **Open and Organized.** It recommends being open to the idea of new strategies and discusses how being organized can help with living a less stressful life. Strategies to improve organization are introduced, as well as ways to study more effectively.

- Chapter 6 is about **Recognize, Relax, and Reflect.** It continues to introduce more mindfulness exercises to help you recognize and engage your senses and relax the body. The idea of monotasking vs. multitasking is also explored.

- Chapter 7 is about **Emotions.** It explains how emotional difficulties are an ever-present reality associated with ADHD, and it also introduces ways that you can manage it.

- Chapter 8 is about **Determination.** That is, the determination to continue to live a mindful life in order to manage the stress and symptoms of ADHD. This chapter also provides a reflection and quick reference guide for what has been introduced throughout the book. Lastly, you'll write a self-care and ANCHORED commitment.

FORMAT FOR EACH CHAPTER

Each chapter begins with an outline that provides an overview of what to expect. Why do we do this? Studies show that previewing a chapter provides a foundation for the material, which, in turn, leads to more information being retained. After the overview is an educational section **(LEARN IT!)**, which introduces information about specific topics. Next, you'll find a section that includes a variety of interventions and strategies **(USE IT!)**. These can include mindfulness of space, body, or mind exercises, or executive functioning exercises. Lastly, you'll encounter the **ANCHOR IT!** section—try not to think of this as the kind of homework you'd encounter in school. Instead, envision this as your first step into practicing skills that will help with several aspects of your life.

It is important that you do not rush this book! Instead, take the time to *incorporate* these exercises into your life. It takes time for new habits to stick, so please be patient and devote at least one week to reading and performing the exercises in each chapter before you move onto the next.

WHAT IS "EXECUTIVE FUNCTIONING" AND HOW IS IT CONNECTED TO ADHD?

Our understanding of ADHD has changed over the years, with the focus shifting from young children to a greater awareness of how the diagnosis affects adolescents and adults. As we learned, adolescence is often reported as the most frustrating time for those with ADHD, often because it is a time when people experience more complex social and academic demands while simultaneously receiving less support from their caregivers and teachers.

Today, we have a better understanding of how **executive functioning** difficulties caused by ADHD complicate a young person's need to plan for both their immediate and long-term futures. You might find that you are having difficulty with organization, planning, getting started on tasks, studying effectively and efficiently, having appropriate emotional responses to situations and experiences, sustaining focus, or some combination of all of the above. While most people have difficulty with the above tasks at some point in their lives, a person with ADHD has *chronic* impairments in these areas. Research has shown that people with ADHD are about twice as likely to struggle with issues of executive functioning as people in the general population.

The executive functions are responsible for helping people perform day-to-day tasks and responsibilities, and each executive function can be traced to specific regions in the brain.

The exercises presented in this workbook will help you improve your executive functioning skills, which will, in turn, reduce stress in your life. These exercises may also help with your academic and personal performance, leading you to experience greater fulfillment and enjoyment. More details about how to mindfully integrate these exercises into your life will be explained in Chapter 2.

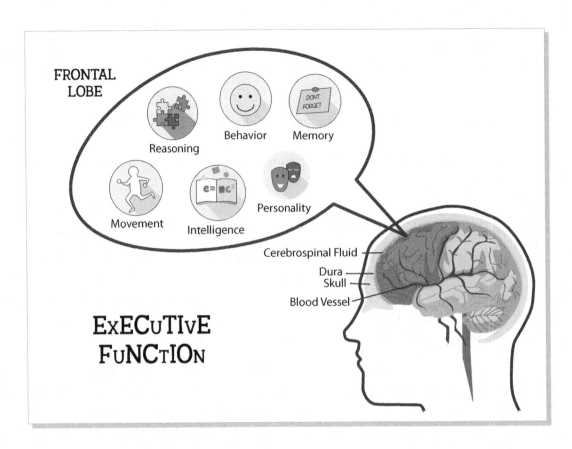

TIME MANAGEMENT/ORGANIZATION EXERCISE: HOW FULL IS YOUR PLATE?

In this day and age, many people simply have too much on their plate. That lack of balance leads to unnecessary stress, which can, in turn, lead to academic and relational difficulties. It can also lead to more difficulty focusing, especially if you become preoccupied about what you cannot do because you don't have time! Living a balanced life can help people become calmer and happier, which are the keys to an *enjoyable* life. It is important to look at what's on <u>your</u> plate so that you understand where your time is being spent and how to better manage it.

wORkSHeET:
How Full is Your Plate?

Using the circle create a pie chart and label how your time is spent. Include things like school, homework, sports, family, friends, fun, etc.

Copyright © 2019, Melissa Springstead Cahill. *ADHD in Teens & Young Adults*. All rights reserved.

After you finish the pie chart, reflect on what you learned by answering the following questions:

How is your time filled?

_____

_____

Do you want to change it?

_____

_____

….If so, what do you want to change?

_____

_____

Is there anything else you want to include in your schedule?

_____

_____

….If so, how do you think you could add it into your schedule?

_____

_____

This exercise can be done any time you feel that you are missing out on something, or during times where you might feel unbalanced or frustrated with how your time is being spent. In the next chapter, we will look more critically at scheduling activities and reflect on the time filled out on your plate.

TIP: Remember that sometimes our schedules are going to be more unbalanced than at other times. If this is a temporary imbalance, be patient and recognize that it _is_ temporary.

Copyright © 2019, Melissa Springstead Cahill. *ADHD in Teens & Young Adults*. All rights reserved.

CASE STUDY – From Teens Like You!

"I remember in my junior year, I wanted to do as much as possible. I was running on the track team, trying to compete in the academic decathlon, taking AP classes, and signing up for school plays. I didn't want to feel like I was missing out on high school or that I had skipped an opportunity to make myself look like a better college applicant. The problem was that my life felt out of control, and I was fighting with my parents constantly about how I was spending my time or when I was going to bed.

When Melissa had me complete the 'How Full is Your Plate?' exercise, I was amazed by how little time there was for me during the day. Every minute put pressure and expectations on me in some way. The plate showed me there was NO balance in my life. Showing this to my parents also let them see that I wasn't just being lazy or dramatic: I really was struggling with over-commitment!

At the beginning of my senior year, I sat down with my mom and dad, and planned the upcoming year with the plate method. That made all of the difference. Now, I can say that this year has been much less stressful and more balanced because I can make sure to have time for myself, chores, schoolwork, and extracurriculars."

– J.S., 17

When we have busy schedules, it can be hard to find the reason why we would want to add *more* to our plate, such as the process of completing this workbook. By having an intention, or an internal sense of "why," it can become easier. In other words, we can gain more from the activities or tasks we originally felt we "didn't have time for." With that in mind, fill out the questions on the following page, providing enough time to reflect on why you decided to progress through this workbook. Think deeply and answer honestly!

wORkSHeET:
Intentions for Learning
and Using ANCHORED

Why have you chosen to complete this ANCHORED workbook? If <u>you</u> did not choose to do so, then explain why someone else might have chosen for you to work on this book.

_____

_____

_____

_____

_____

What do you hope to gain from completing this ANCHORED workbook? If you aren't sure, then feel free to write down some aspects of your life that you wish were easier or less stressful.

_____

_____

_____

_____

_____

_____

Copyright © 2019, Melissa Springstead Cahill. *ADHD in Teens & Young Adults*. All rights reserved.

INTENTIONS VS. GOAL SETTING

All human beings set goals, and young people like yourself are often expected to set goals in many areas of their life. For example, we might set a goal of making a sports team, a goal of going to a favorite college, or anything that has to do with the future. While it is important for all people to have a reason *why* they are doing something, a person with ADHD has a much more difficult time working towards a goal when it seems like the "why" is missing. Establishing that "why" can help a person become more interested in working toward that goal, which, in turn, leads to more focus. In short, goal setting helps a person create a *plan* to achieve a *want*. It is important to recognize that setting a goal often reveals something that has not been accomplished that is necessary to achieve that goal. For example, let's say your goal is to have a car and the independence that comes with it. If so, you'll probably need to satisfy a number of smaller requirements, such as saving up money through a summer job and passing your driver's test.

Oftentimes, if that missing "something" is not accomplished within the constraints under which that goal was set, it can lead people to experience a sense of failure and, in turn, cause them to feel as if they are a failure overall. **It is for this reason that people sometimes refuse to set goals: They're afraid of disappointing themselves.** In the short term, this kind of thinking protects a person's ego, but over the long term, it can deprive people of the valuable growth and experience they need to be a complete person. Goal setting is important, but it certainly isn't easy and often doesn't come naturally to most people.

Consider also that when people set goals, they are focusing on what they feel is missing, rather than forming a plan that will lead to future self-improvement or happiness. For example, if a student sets a goal that sounds like, "I want to raise my grades," it avoids asking the question, "Are my grades currently acceptable? Why or why not?" Goals often carry implicit judgments about where a person happens to be in life, and, often, these judgments are unhealthy.

Setting an **intention** is a more mindful way of goal setting because it allows you to be accepting of where you are in life, rather than focusing on what you have not accomplished, achieved, mastered, etc. An intention could be something like, "I intend for my mind to be open to learning and reflecting on what it means to have ADHD." The *goal* for that same idea might sound like, "I will learn multiple strategies to help with my ADHD." **Consider this: The goal could set you up for failure if it is not achieved, whereas the intention opens up possibilities and allows for something to happen.** For example, rather than setting a goal of "I want to own a car," a teen might set an intention of "I intend to be more independent." Setting daily, weekly, monthly, and yearly intentions can help you to live a happier and more successful life, often leading to the same goals you had hoped to achieve.

Now, I want you to read back through your answers to the earlier questions regarding "Intentions for Learning and Using ANCHORED." See if the language you used sounded more "goal-based" or "intention-based," and check the appropriate "goal" or "intention" box in the following exercise with that in mind. After doing so, fill out the remaining sections of the exercise.

Goal vs. Intention

_____ Goal   _____ Intention

If your answers sounded more like a goal, I want you to try rewriting them into an intention:

_____

_____

_____

Now that you've reflected on the purpose of learning the ANCHORED approach and learned about goals vs. intentions, write a couple of *intentions* you hope to gain in the lines that follow. These can be from this program or for your life in the next day, year, etc.

My ANCHORED Intention:

(That is, what are your intentions for this book, specifically?)

_____

_____

_____

My Personal Daily Intention:

_____

_____

_____

My Personal Yearly Intention:

_____

_____

_____

Copyright © 2019, Melissa Springstead Cahill. *ADHD in Teens & Young Adults*. All rights reserved.

CaSE StUDy — From Teens Like You!

"I first started working with Melissa for help with my depression. I felt like all around me, there were kids who were just flat-out 'better' than I was. In class, I felt like there were better students sitting all around me. After school, it felt like I was competing with girls who were much better dancers, and, at home, I kept comparing myself to my older cousins who had already gotten into good schools.

I became really upset by my lack of recognition and rewards. At a certain point, I found it hard to motivate myself to do anything. I thought if I tried my hardest, I would always just be 'second best.' I also started to feel even worse because I was sad so often. I never felt 'okay,' and I started worrying that I wouldn't ever feel okay. I also felt like my ADHD was holding me back from being successful.

Melissa taught me how to accept where I am in life. The first step was to stop looking at myself through the goals I had set in the past. Changing my thinking from goals to intentions let me think more about who I wanted to be and what kinds of actions I would need to take (one step at a time) to get there. I still struggle with depression, but I feel like every day gets a little better. My intentions help me look at each day positively and see so many opportunities around me."

– K.W., 18

INTRODUCTION TO MINDFULNESS AND DEEP BREATHING EXERCISE

Mindfulness is a technique that helps people change the way they interact with their thoughts and feelings, and it is one of the most helpful components when it comes to managing adolescent impairment due to ADHD. The best way to think about mindfulness is simply as a way of focusing attention. It is a concept that is thousands of years old and stems from the Buddhist practice of meditating. Mindfulness meditation is used for spiritual and intellectual development to help people concentrate better and live more peaceful and accepting lives. As described by Jon Kabat-Zinn, a professor who spent his career crafting mindfulness-based techniques to reduce stress, mindfulness is "the awareness that emerges through paying attention on purpose in the present moment, and non-judgmentally to the unfolding experience moment by moment" (2003, p. 145). **In other words, mindfulness involves fully immersing yourself in whatever you are doing in the present moment without any distractions and without making any evaluative judgments.** For example, when you are eating a meal, you just focus on *eating*. When you are doing homework, you just focus on *working*. When you are having a conversation with a friend, you just focus on *talking with that person*. The point is to completely participate in whatever is occurring in the present moment without judging it as "good" or "bad," or without focusing on the "shoulds" or "should nots."

Mindfulness interventions are not only beneficial to adolescents with ADHD—they can be of great benefit to parents and caregivers as well. If you are a person reading this book in order to help support a teen in your life, I would recommend that you take on the task of doing the mindfulness exercises in this book as well. For example, you could implement a daily mindfulness exercise time for the family, or at least schedule time to do so a few days each week. Don't force it, but if your family is open and receptive, then it could be a big help in creating a routine and connecting the family. Mindfulness will be explained in more detail in Chapter 2.

Deep Breathing

For this first week, you will be practicing deep breathing (also called abdominal breathing, diaphragmatic breathing, or belly breathing). When people are taught breathing exercises, they are often incorrectly told to suck in their stomach or to engage their core. When doing this, the breath becomes shallow and is only done through the chest, which leads to an increase in tension and anxiety. If that's what you've been told deep breathing is, forget what you know—we'll be learning a new way.

The correct method of deep breathing can feel a little bit unnatural due to the fact that the belly no longer remains flat, but instead rises and falls with each breath. True deep breathing allows for oxygenated air to come in and carbon dioxide to go out. This process can help slow the heartbeat and stabilize blood pressure. It is important to have oxygenated air reach the lowest part of the lungs to help increase feelings of calm and to help decrease distracting thoughts. We're going to practice how to do this right now.

Introduction to Breathing

Place one hand on the chest and one on the lower belly.

Slowly breathe in through your nose, allowing your chest and lower belly to rise, and fill your lungs.

Relax your belly and allow for it to expand fully.

Now, breathe out slowly through your mouth, allowing your chest and lower belly to fall.

Once you have practiced breathing like this a few times, set a timer (not an alarm—a meditation bell is recommended) for three minutes.

During this time, sit or lay comfortably with your feet on the ground and your eyes closed (if you prefer to have them open, then find a spot in front of you that you can stare into to minimize any visual distractions).

Breathe this way until the timer goes off.

TIP: My recommendation:
Download a sound bowl meditation app that you can use as a timer.
The sound is gentler and can help keep your body in a relaxed state.

Copyright © 2019, Melissa Springstead Cahill. *ADHD in Teens & Young Adults*. All rights reserved.

MiNDfULnESs ExERcISe:
Deep Breathing

Once you have practiced the introduction to breathing, try the following deep breathing meditation exercise.

Deep Breathing Meditation

Time: 3 minutes

Sit in a comfortable position with your back away from your chair so you are supporting your spine on your own.

Place your feet on the ground.

Rest your hands in your lap or on your knees. You may also try placing one hand on your chest and one hand on your lower abdomen so you can feel your breath rise and fall in your body.

- **Notice your body.** Sit comfortably but alert. Your shoulders and hips should be relaxed, and your feet should be touching the floor. Close your eyes.

- **Notice your breath.** Inhale through your nose. Exhale comfortably through the nose, the nose and the mouth, or the mouth only. Notice the rise and fall of your breath in and out of your body. If it helps, you may inhale to a count of four, and exhale to a count of four to eight.

- **Notice what happens.**

  – **Thoughts:** Are you thinking? What are you thinking about? Is your mind wandering? Daydreaming? Making a to-do list? Having memories from something that happened recently or long ago?

  – **Feelings:** What are you feeling? Do you notice any emotions, good or bad?

  – **Sensations:** What do you feel in your body? Is it pleasant? Unpleasant? Neither? Are you feeling achy or tense? Are some areas relaxed?

  – Continue breathing while saying to yourself, "Breathing in, I calm my mind and body. Breathing out, I release what I am holding in my mind and body."

Adapted from Kabat-Zinn (1990)

Copyright © 2019, Melissa Springstead Cahill. *ADHD in Teens & Young Adults*. All rights reserved.

ANCHOR IT!

- *Mindfulness Meditation Tracking Sheet*

- Practice this breathing exercise daily, if possible. If you are not able to practice on a certain day, then make a point to tackle it the next day.

- Another tip: Set an alert reminder on your phone to go off at the same time each day. Being able to practice the breathing exercise at the same time each day will help to create a habit that won't be as easily forgotten.

- On the next page there is a tracking sheet to help you reflect on your experience during the breathing exercise. It can also help to show the progress you are making in taking an active role in living a more productive, calm, and happy life.

- Look over the sample tracking sheet I have provided to familiarize yourself with it. Then print a blank tracking sheet and keep it available for you to use in the following weeks.

<u>Sample</u>

Mindfulness Meditation Tracking Sheet

Week of: February 19

DAY/DATE	DID YOU PRACTICE?	COMMENTS
Monday 2/19	Yes	I noticed worrying about getting to my homework.
Tuesday 2/20	No	I forgot.
Wednesday 2/21	No	Maybe setting a reminder is a good idea!
Thursday 2/22	Yes	Reminder helped (even if I had to snooze it a bit!). I noticed tension in my shoulders while thinking about my soccer game tomorrow.
Friday 2/23	Yes	I almost forgot but remembered right before bed. This was easier, and I noticed my body calming/tension going away a little bit.

Mindfulness Meditation Tracking Sheet

Week of: _____

DAY/DATE	DID YOU PRACTICE?	COMMENTS

Copyright © 2019, Melissa Springstead Cahill. *ADHD in Teens & Young Adults*. All rights reserved.

CHAPTER 2

N: Natural Awareness

LEARN IT!
- More About Mindfulness
- Levels of Mindfulness

USE IT!
- Mindfulness Exercises:
    - *Mindful vs. Mindless/Autopilot!*
    - *Mindful Eating*
- Time Management and Organization: *Weekly Schedule*

ANCHOR IT!
- Mindfulness Meditation Tracking Sheet
- Mindful Awareness of Eating
- Weekly Schedule

MORE ABOUT MINDFULNESS

We talked generally about **mindfulness** in the last chapter. Here, we're going to make it the star of the show. Mindfulness can actually become a clinical approach to help a person respond to stress and emotional distress. It is an approach in which a person pays attention, on purpose, to what is happening in the present moment. Although meditation is a formal intervention that is commonly used to increase mindfulness, the concept of mindfulness is not limited to meditation. Rather, mindfulness involves a set of techniques that are used to increase the degree to which we are fully present and aware in our everyday lives.

As a psychological process, mindfulness is developed over time and with practice. It involves consciously attempting to increase focus on thoughts and draw attention to the "here and now" without analyzing or reacting in a habitual, automatic way. Rather, it involves just noticing whatever thoughts, feelings, or sensations may arise in the moment without trying to fight against them or change them in any way. Skills can be acquired to allow a person to be mindful in many situations and to respond to what are normally emotional situations in a calmer manner. It requires an open, non-judgmental mind that is aware and accepting of the present moment—one that resists the temptation and desire to get stuck in whatever thoughts and feelings may arise. A goal of mindfulness meditation is to become aware and non-reactive in the present moment.

By observing and paying attention to thoughts, feelings, and sensations that are happening moment to moment, a person is alert and fully present. Acknowledging feelings, thoughts, and sensations while using deep breathing is a vital tool that helps you remain mindful. It is not a practice of *suppressing* your thoughts but, instead, of observing them and allowing them to move on rather than holding onto them.

There are three primary elements of mindfulness: attitude, attention, and intention.

- **Attitude** consists of being non-judgmental, patient, accepting, trusting, and having a beginner's mind. It is also important to be kind to yourself and to minimize judgmental thoughts and feelings. However, if you find yourself making judgments, don't judge your judging! Just notice the judgments, take a deep breath, and try to accept and place trust in your experience.

- **Attention** consists of focusing and being able to recognize when the mind wanders. It involves being curious about what your thoughts, feelings, and emotions are. It requires pausing, focusing on taking a deep breath, and having an awareness of the sensations in your body.

- **Intention** refers to the commitment to let go of the distracting thoughts that prevent you from connecting to your body. In order to gain this skill, it is important to incorporate mindfulness exercises into your daily routine. If you'd like, you can go back to Chapter 1 and include a mindfulness intention in your "My Intention" exercise.

The heart of mindfulness practice is to observe your own experiences, acknowledge that they are occurring, and put them to the side while you focus attention on your breathing. Be curious about where the mind wanders and about the experience you have at any moment. Do not try to take a stance on your thoughts, feelings, or sensations. Instead, just notice them as they come into consciousness and accept them as they are. Acceptance means that a person is open to the present moment and does not have an agenda about their experiences. Rather, the person allows him or herself to be open and receptive to any experience.

Using the breath as an anchor helps you to focus on the "here and now" in day-to-day life, which will help you reduce your worries and overthinking of thoughts. Attitude, attention, and intention are all interconnected, and they all happen simultaneously in the process of mindfulness. When you are mindful, you'll find that you are a better witness to experiences, which will allow you to think and act in a more reflective and deliberate way over time.

TIP: Think about mindfulness as a way to calm your mind
so that you can be more relaxed and more attentive.

LEVELS OF MINDFULNESS: SPACE, BODY, AND MIND

In this book, you will learn exercises that focus on space, body, and mind. *Mindfulness of Space* refers to focusing on what is happening outside of your body. For example, paying attention to the literal space around you and the time of day. *Mindfulness of Body* refers to your feelings and emotions, such as asking what you feel in your body, both physically and emotionally. *Mindfulness of Mind* refers to the thoughts you have. It can refer to the levels of clutter you feel with thoughts bouncing around, as well as your feelings of being overwhelmed with stress and anxiety. Each of these are connected, and some experiences can fit into multiple levels.

Mindful vs. Mindless/Autopilot

Set a timer for one minute (use a meditation bell if you have it on an app). Start by finding a comfortable position. When you are ready, start the timer. Feel free to close your eyes if that's comfortable for you. If not, then just let your gaze soften and rest on the floor in front of you. Remain seated like this until your timer goes off.

What did you notice?

_____

_____

What did you hear?

_____

_____

Let's do this again, but this time, pay very close attention to all the sounds that come and go. Notice sounds that are close to you, as well as sounds that are farther away. Notice how they appear and then disappear.

What did you notice?

_____

_____

What did you hear?

_____

_____

How was the first listening different from the second?

_____

_____

This exercise is an example of how you begin to cultivate mindfulness. You paid attention, on purpose, to what was happening in the present moment. It was also important to be open, interested, curious, and without judgment in the present moment—these are all a foundational part of mindfulness.

You may not have heard *all* the sounds unfolding around you in the first listening exercise. If so, this is an example of doing things on autopilot without full awareness. When a person

Copyright © 2019, Melissa Springstead Cahill. *ADHD in Teens & Young Adults*. All rights reserved.

doesn't have that full awareness, we call it a state of being "mindless." You possibly heard more sounds on the second listening exercise since it was pointed out for you to do so. This exercise is the opposite of being mindless or on autopilot, and it is an example of being mindful. Think about things that you have done mindfully recently. Do you remember what you ate during your last meal, or what color the flowers were outside your school today?

Write down some examples of things that you do in your everyday life that are mindless. Some examples could be eating a meal, brushing your teeth, or walking to your classroom.

Mindless Activities:

_____

_____

_____

Now, write down some examples of things that you do in your everyday life that are mindful. These are things that you have to pay attention to and focus on. These can be things that are not habits, or things you are currently learning, such as driving lessons.

Mindful Activities:

_____

_____

_____

Was that easy to do? Was it easier or harder to come up with mindful or mindless activities? The more we practice being mindful in daily activities, the more our brain is naturally able to be present in our day-to-day experiences. We will further explore mindfulness throughout this book.

Copyright © 2019, Melissa Springstead Cahill. *ADHD in Teens & Young Adults*. All rights reserved.

MiNDfULnESs ExERcISe:
Mindful Eating

Eating is an everyday activity that you can use as a way to practice mindfulness. A common food used in the mindful eating exercise is a raisin, but feel free to use something else. Whatever you use, make sure to have two or three of them. You can do the following exercise several times in order to see if you notice anything different each time. This mindfulness exercise will also continue to help you to remain focused more easily in other areas of your life.

Instructions: Sitting comfortably in a chair, look at the raisins as if you have never seen them before. Imagine you have arrived from another planet and the raisin is completely new to you. Take the raisin and turn it around. Look at its shape, texture, color, size, temperature, hardness, and softness. If you find that you are thinking about something else, just notice each thought as it arrives and let it go, bringing your attention back to the raisin.

Now, being aware of the movement of your arm, bring the raisin to your nose and smell it. Place it into your mouth, without chewing or swallowing. Pay attention to all the sensations: texture, taste, shape. When you are ready, take a bite and notice the change. Notice the new texture. Notice the rest of your mouth. Notice every sensation you can. Now, slowly and consciously chew the raisin.

When you are ready, swallow.

Once you are finished with the mindful eating exercise, reflect on the following questions:

What did you notice? Smell? Texture? Taste?

_____

_____

What was it like to hold something in your mouth without eating it?

_____

_____

Where was your attention? What happened when it wandered?

_____

_____

Try to remember this experience, and try at least once a day to have a mindful eating experience. You may notice that you enjoy foods differently, or perhaps that you are more easily satisfied. Allow and accept whatever the experience is for you.

Copyright © 2019, Melissa Springstead Cahill. *ADHD in Teens & Young Adults*. All rights reserved.

TIME MANAGEMENT AND ORGANIZATION: WEEKLY SCHEDULE

In Chapter 1, you did an activity to gauge how full your plate is. As you learned through that exercise, balance is important in order to live mindful, focused, happy, and fulfilled lives. For adolescents who have ADHD—and, in turn, difficulties with executive functioning—it is particularly important to implement time management and organizational skills to find this balance. Keeping organized and effectively managing one's time not only helps with academics, but it benefits social interactions and other day-to-day tasks as well. When you have difficulty keeping track of time, life in general becomes more difficult to manage, which can lead to failure in school, in the workplace, and interpersonally.

Remember, managing your time and being organized is another way of being mindful. By being more organized when it comes to your time, your space, and your belongings, it will be easier to be more mindful in other activities. And don't worry, later chapters will give you tips and exercises for exactly how to become organized!

With that in mind, it is helpful to bring attention to time in order to help you slow down—sometimes, to pause entirely—and then reflect on what is happening or should be happening. Since time is abstract and unable to be seen, it is important to teach you how to use a few tools that will help make it concrete and visible.

While time-focused strategies can help you with homework completion, it is also important to understand the importance of reducing distractions. Almost always, that means not multitasking during homework and study time. As an adolescent, you tend to have multiple distractions, ranging from social media, email, phone notifications, music, or simply eating a snack. The teenage brain will trick you into thinking that you are not negatively affected by multitasking, but it is known that the brain can only efficiently do one thing at a time. And if someone *can* effectively and successfully multitask, it is evidence that they have an above average **working memory**—that is, a system for temporarily storing and managing the information required to carry out complex cognitive tasks such as learning, reasoning, and comprehension. In contrast, ADHD tends to result in difficulties with working memory, so it is important to understand that you can complete homework faster and more successfully when you are <u>not</u> multitasking. We will get into more about multitasking vs. monotasking and deal with homework in Chapter 4.

Let's get started by thinking about how you spend your time in a given week. Think about school, studying, homework, and extracurricular activities. Do you have set times for any of these activities? If so, put the times on the following spreadsheet. If not, can you estimate how much time is or should be spent on each activity?

TIP: When a person feels more organized with managing time,
they often feel more successful, leading to an increase in self-esteem.
Visual tools can help strengthen executive functioning skills.

Once you have the spreadsheet filled out with your schedule, go over it with someone who might currently help you with scheduling activities. Maybe a parent or caregiver? Make sure that any fixed weekly appointments are listed. It is important to also be aware that things always come up that we don't plan for. For that reason, it is important to have some flexibility in your schedule to allow for life to happen without it causing too much extra stress. Brainstorm what might come up for you on a periodic basis—things like family dinners, birthday parties, make-up work from being sick, etc. What are some other things that may come up but do not happen weekly?

How Do I Spend My Time?

Day	Activity	Times
Example: Wednesday	School Theatre Rehearsal Homework Dinner TV Show Shower	8 a.m. – 3 p.m. 3:30 p.m. – 5:30 p.m. Varies After rehearsal, but maybe also after doing some homework 9 p.m. (but can record) Before bed? Or morning?
Example: Sunday	Math Tutor Homework	6:30 p.m. – 8 p.m. Varies – want to be finished by 6 p.m.
Monday		
Tuesday		
Wednesday		
Thursday		
Friday		
Saturday		
Sunday		

Copyright © 2019, Melissa Springstead Cahill. *ADHD in Teens & Young Adults*. All rights reserved.

Weekly Schedule

Now, you are ready to plan out your schedule on the following **Weekly Schedule** handout. Using the ***How Do I Spend My Time?*** spreadsheet as a reference, take a couple of colored pens and write/shade in the time slots that are already accounted for on a weekly basis. Do not fill in any activities that are not set in stone. Those can be scheduled on a week-by-week or day-by-day basis. Once you have a foundation for where your time is being spent, you can start to see what extra time you have, which might allow you to see if anything could be changed around to give you a more efficient use of your time.

wORkSHEET: Weekly Schedule

Monday	Tuesday	Wednesday	Thursday	Friday	Saturday	Sunday
6 am	6 am	6 am	6 am	6 am	6 am	6 am
7 am	7 am	7 am	7 am	7 am	7 am	7 am
8 am	8 am	8 am	8 am	8 am	8 am	8 am
9 am	9 am	9 am	9 am	9 am	9 am	9 am
10 am	10 am	10 am	10 am	10 am	10 am	10 am
11 am	11 am	11 am	11 am	11 am	11 am	11 am
12 pm	12 pm	12 pm	12 pm	12 pm	12 pm	12 pm
1 pm	1 pm	1 pm	1 pm	1 pm	1 pm	1 pm
2 pm	2 pm	2 pm	2 pm	2 pm	2 pm	2 pm
3 pm	3 pm	3 pm	3 pm	3 pm	3 pm	3 pm
4 pm	4 pm	4 pm	4 pm	4 pm	4 pm	4 pm
5 pm	5 pm	5 pm	5 pm	5 pm	5 pm	5 pm
6 pm	6 pm	6 pm	6 pm	6 pm	6 pm	6 pm
7 pm	7 pm	7 pm	7 pm	7 pm	7 pm	7 pm
8 pm	8 pm	8 pm	8 pm	8 pm	8 pm	8 pm
9 pm	9 pm	9 pm	9 pm	9 pm	9 pm	9 pm
10 pm	10 pm	10 pm	10 pm	10 pm	10 pm	10 pm

Copyright © 2019, Melissa Springstead Cahill. *ADHD in Teens & Young Adults*. All rights reserved.

Often, homework is an activity that is not scheduled. It is assumed that it will be done at any time after school and before bed. However, if you are not mindful about scheduling time for homework, you could end up doing homework during all of your free time, leading to a lack of balance in life. It is important to spend time scheduling homework each week to help prevent unintended stress due to inevitable surprises. Some things to think about before scheduling your homework time:

- How long *should* homework take you on a nightly basis?
- Is it different from day to day?

Looking at your *Weekly Schedule*, write down blocks of time for homework. You will do an exercise about time in Chapter 3 to help you obtain a more accurate idea of how long homework will take.

TIP: Balance is important, so try to schedule homework so that you can also have unstructured down time.

Once you have your *Weekly Schedule* filled out, make sure you have some blank sheets on hand, as well as a copy of your current schedule. If you have not gone over it with a parent/caregiver, make sure to do that so that you can limit any surprises during your week. Now that you have learned more about mindfulness and how it can help you, is there anything on your schedule that you could do more mindfully? If so, highlight that activity in yellow. It would also be helpful to add your daily mindfulness practice onto the schedule. It is recommended that you add it during the morning and/or evening. For now, just keep doing the deep belly breathing that was described in Chapter 1. As you learn more strategies, you can start to incorporate those as well!

CaSE StUDy — From Teens Like You!

"I love my parents, but 'family dinner time' started turning into a big issue. When dinner was ready, we all needed to sit down at the table as a family and spend time together. However, this became a problem in high school when it would feel like I was being called to the table right when I was right in the middle of something. Always!

Before long, I was fighting with my parents and my sister about it. They would say that dinner time is basically the same time every day, so why was it an issue? I told them that they had no idea what it was like to finally find focus and then have someone yank you away. Meanwhile, I found I was staying up later and having a lot of anxiety anytime anything unexpected came up. I would get my homework done, but sometimes I would fall asleep at 3 a.m.

Making a weekly schedule helped me to understand how a lot of my stress came from my constantly thinking I had more time to get things done. I started to see how much time I had for myself and my schoolwork, and when I needed to be available for my family. Committing to the planner has not only let me make better use of my time, but I finally look forward to dinner again!"

– E.M., 16

ANCHOR IT!

For this week, you'll be using three tools we've learned together:

- *Mindfulness Meditation Tracking Sheet*
  - An additional mindful breathing meditation script follows this chapter. You can have someone close to you record their voice reading the script.

- *Mindful Awareness of Eating:* This will help you become aware of what you notice when eating (for example: tastes, sights, smells, and body sensations).
  - Each day this week, eat at least one meal (or part of a meal), paying attention in the same way as you did during the raisin exercise.

- Use the *Weekly Schedule* for scheduling homework and reminders for your mindfulness exercise.

wORkSHeET:
Mindfulness Meditation Script

Time: 3 minutes

Let's start with a few minutes of mindfulness practice. Feel free to close your eyes if that is comfortable for you. You may also allow your eyes to have a soft gaze on the floor in front of you. Let go of anything you might be holding.

Find a comfortable position in your chair, with your back straight, but not stiff. Your shoulders should be relaxed, along with your face muscles, and your hands should rest comfortably on your thighs or lap.

Pause.

Now, take a deep breath through your nose, and let the breath come out through your mouth. Try to let your breath out slow and long with a slight sound. Do this two or three more times.

Pause.

Now, let your breath move in and out of your nostrils soundlessly. Just pay attention to the in-breath and the out-breath.

Pause.

There is only one thing to do right now: Feel your breath move. Notice the sensations of your breathing.

Pause.

Pay attention to the in-breath and the out-breath until you hear the sound of the bell.

Copyright © 2019, Melissa Springstead Cahill. *ADHD in Teens & Young Adults.* All rights reserved.

wORkSHeET:
Mindfulness Meditation Tracking Sheet

Week of: _____

DAY/DATE	DID YOU PRACTICE?	COMMENTS

Copyright © 2019, Melissa Springstead Cahill. *ADHD in Teens & Young Adults*. All rights reserved.

C: Concentrate on Purpose

LEARN IT!

- Concentration and Focus: How Does Mindfulness Help with Concentration?

USE IT!

- Mindfulness Exercises:
    - *My World Around Me!*
    - *Routine Activities*
- Managing Time: *Homework Organizer*
- Mindfulness Exercise: *S.T.O.P.*

ANCHOR IT!

- *Mindfulness Meditation Tracking Sheet*
- *Routine Activities*
- *Homework Organizer*

CONCENTRATION AND FOCUS: HOW DOES MINDFULNESS HELP WITH CONCENTRATION?

Mindfulness can be described as a type of training that helps boost your attention, cognitive, and self-control resources. The more you practice being mindful, the more you strengthen the parts of the brain that are responsible for executive functioning—the same parts, incidentally, that are most often impacted by ADHD. The following section describes executive functioning and the support that mindfulness practice can bring.

Attention. People with ADHD often have a hard time focusing and paying attention when they need to. For example, you might become hyper-focused when completing an interesting or engaging task, which makes it difficult for you to recognize when it is time to stop that task and move onto the next. Alternatively, you might struggle to remain focused on other activities that are more mundane or less stimulating but that you need to complete anyway. Mindfulness practice helps address this issue by helping you become more aware of your attention, leading to success in focusing when needed. For example, the breathing exercise you are working on now is a mindfulness exercise that can help you to become more alert. When you recognize that you are distracted, try to focus on your breath, bringing your attention back to the present moment and place.

Memory. ADHD often causes difficulty in working memory—which is another executive function. Working memory is sometimes called "memory in action," since it's often used while you're in the middle of an activity. For example, if someone ever told you a phone number to dial, and you continued to repeat it to yourself as you punched in the numbers, in that moment you were using your working memory. When you learn something new, your working memory temporarily holds that information in your mind and tries linking it to something you have already stored. This process can make it easier to retrieve that information later. For example, when trying to remember a new teacher's name, you might link it to a familiar object or image. If your teacher's name is Mr. Green, you might think of a field of green grass. Only then will you be able to move the information out of your working memory and into long-term memory.

When an adolescent with ADHD has difficulty with working memory, it can make it hard to learn and remember what is taught in school. Mindfulness practice engages your working memory by helping you remember what to do when you recognize that your mind has wandered off, or when you realize that you are off task. When a person is engaged in mindfulness practice, their working memory is also engaged.

Emotion Regulation. Emotion regulation, which is the ability to balance and control emotions, is another aspect of life that is difficult for a person with ADHD. When you have well-developed emotion regulation skills, you can effectively control your emotions and/or impulses. In contrast, if you have problems regulating your emotions, you can become more easily frustrated and have more difficulty calming yourself down, which can lead you to act out on your impulses. Mindfulness can improve your emotion regulation skills by helping you become more aware of your feelings without pushing them away or feeling like you are being flooded. It can also help reduce impulsiveness.

A practice that helps with emotion regulation involves labeling your feelings, or putting a name to an experience, in a non-judgmental way. Being non-judgmental involves simply describing what you are observing in an objective, non-biased manner—in wording that even others would agree with. For example, you would describe a feeling for what it is (e.g., "just a feeling") without labeling it as "right" or "wrong." This strategy can help you respond constructively to a situation instead of reacting in an overly emotional or impulsive way.

Coping with Stress. Although stress is a common issue that everyone will experience in their lives, adolescents these days are experiencing more stress than in the past. For those with ADHD, this stress is often compounded by the difficulties that their symptoms play in preventing them from experiencing a high quality of life. Mindfulness practice can reduce the physiological impact of ongoing stress by helping your body to relax. It can also help you experience more positive emotions, which, in turn, helps you to be more self-accepting. This can lead to an improvement in body and brain functioning.

MiNDfULnESs ExERcISe:
My World Around Me!

As we learned in the last chapter, it's easy to be mindless. We often go through life on autopilot, not recognizing what is around us.

The following exercise is an example of something that can help us to pause and become more connected to our environment. As I mentioned previously, the more you practice mindfulness exercises, the easier it becomes to pay attention in other areas of your life.

For this activity, I want you to take a minute and think about where you are.

Are you in your house?

A public place?

If you're in your house, where are you, specifically?

Now, if possible, I want you to walk outside of the area you are in, bringing this book, along with a pencil or pen. You could go to another area of the house, or outside your front or back door. If you're in a public area, you could move to another part of that space. Or, if none of that is possible, you can stay where you are. However, once you find a new area of interest, mindfully observe what you are looking at.

Copyright © 2019, Melissa Springstead Cahill. *ADHD in Teens & Young Adults*. All rights reserved.

My World Around Me!

What do I see?

_____

_____

_____

What is its shape, color, texture?

_____

_____

_____

Does it move? How?

_____

_____

_____

Is it small? Big?

_____

_____

_____

What other things do I sense (hear, smell, etc.)?

_____

_____

_____

Draw what you see on the following blank page.

Copyright © 2019, Melissa Springstead Cahill. *ADHD in Teens & Young Adults*. All rights reserved.

wORkSHeET:
Drawing Page

Copyright © 2019, Melissa Springstead Cahill. *ADHD in Teens & Young Adults*. All rights reserved.

wORkSHeET:
Routine Activities

Every day, we participate in routine activities—typically on autopilot. By bringing a mindful awareness to these routine activities, we are choosing to concentrate on purpose, leading to more focused attention. This next exercise is another example of how we can pay attention to what we are doing, leading to an increase in concentration. Pick one routine activity from the following list or write your own.

Pick one of the activities below to experiment with over the next week:

_____ Showering	_____ Getting ready for bed
_____ Washing your face	_____ Brushing your teeth
_____ Using social media	_____ Texting
_____ Getting dressed	_____ Eating a meal
_____ Driving to school	_____ Driving in the car
_____ Packing your backpack	_____ Other:

Don't forget to set or place a reminder!

Over the next week, try to be *connected* to what you are doing. For example, if you are brushing your teeth, try to focus on the sensation of the brush, tasting the toothpaste, and counting how long you brush in each section of the mouth. Another example is if you are washing your hair, feel the shampoo suds, and then feel the water rinsing them off.

One way to fast-track mindfulness in routine activities is to give yourself visual reminders. Consider putting colored stickers in various places for routine activities. You can put one on the refrigerator to remind you to be mindful when eating. You can put one on the bathroom mirror to remind you to be mindful when brushing your teeth. Remember, it is not yet a *habit* to perform these day-to-day activities mindfully, which means you need help to be successful! Think about where else you can put stickers and write them here:

1. _____

2. _____

3. _____

4. _____

5. _____

6. _____

> TIP: In addition to the stickers, you can also set an alert or a reminder on your phone, tablet, or computer to remember to try to perform any given activity mindfully.

Copyright © 2019, Melissa Springstead Cahill. *ADHD in Teens & Young Adults*. All rights reserved.

MANAGING TIME: THE HOMEWORK ORGANIZER

When you have difficulty concentrating, it can often make it hard to manage your time. This can be especially frustrating when it comes to homework and studying. With the amount of time spent in school and doing extracurricular activities, it is important to have a good idea of how long homework and other tasks are taking. Being able to estimate how long these tasks take will allow you to schedule other fun things and also have some down time. We all have an idea in our mind, often subconsciously, about how long a task will take to complete. Sometimes this is accurate, and other times it is not.

I like to think of this as a battle between our internal clock and our external (or actual) clock. Your internal clock may say to you and your parents that you have "only a little homework," so you run errands, go out to dinner, etc. You then come home and begin working on your homework, at which point you realize that it will actually take you a lot longer! Sometimes your parents will then get mad, thinking that you "lied," when, in actuality, you just lacked an accurate internal clock. The ***Homework Organizer*** is a tool that helps exercise your internal clock so that it matches the actual clock.

How to use the ***Homework Organizer***:

- Fill out one line for each homework assignment.
    - Do not put multiple assignments for one subject on the same line. For example, if you have three things to do for Math, write them separately.
- Then, write the due date. Is it due tomorrow or at a later time?
- Estimate how long you think each task will take. If it is longer than one hour, see if you can break the assignment into parts.
- Now that you have written everything down, add up the estimated time to get an idea of how long you need for homework.
- Take a look at your ***Weekly Schedule*** (Chapter 2) and see what times you have allotted for completing homework.
- Now, fill out the priority column to determine the order that you will be completing your homework. If you know that you will have a late night, then try to take advantage of small breaks. For example, if you have a small break between school and sports, maybe you can do a smaller assignment then.

TIP: If you can, do the harder assignments first!
You will be more rested and focused!

SaMPLE Homework Organizer

Priority	Subject	Assignment	Due Date	Estimated Time	Actual Time	Completed
1	History	Read Chapter 7	1/10	30 min	41 min	Yes
2	History	Answer Chapter 7 questions	1/10	30 min	27 min	Yes
3	English	Annotate readings	1/10	45 min	33 min	Yes
4	English	Discussion questions	1/10	45 min	55 min	No
5	Science	Read Chapter 2	1/11	30 min	30 min	Yes
6	Math	Page 19 #2–36 Even	1/11	30 min	46 min	Yes
7	Math	Test on Chapter 2	1/18	–	–	Yes
8	Math	Email teacher to meet about test	1/11	5 min	2 min	Yes

Copyright © 2019, Melissa Springstead Cahill. *ADHD in Teens & Young Adults*. All rights reserved.

Try to fill out the ***Homework Organizer*** right as the school day ends, when all the tasks you need to complete are the freshest in your mind. If that is not possible, then fill it out once you get home, before doing anything else! This will help you to plan the rest of your evening more effectively. Make sure to keep your ***Weekly Schedule*** nearby to help with planning out your homework. Consider experimenting to see if certain days are easier or harder to do homework. Are there days that you are really busy (so you may be more tired), and homework then takes longer? Can you work ahead or give yourself a night off?

For each assignment you begin, make sure you have something to time yourself with. You'll want to use a stopwatch feature because you'll want to know the *exact* time each task took you to complete (not an estimate). If you use your phone or tablet, try putting it in airplane mode to see if it takes you less time to complete each task when your notifications do not come in!

Since you are timing yourself, you don't want to have to get up during an assignment. If you have a long task, you may want to see if you can break it into two or three smaller assignments. So, before starting each assignment, do a check-in: Do I need to use the restroom? Do I need a drink of water? Again, time each assignment separately. When finished, write the actual time it took. Then move on to the next assignment. Do this each day, and see if you notice any change in your estimated time vs. your actual time.

Go ahead and fill out a ***Homework Organizer*** worksheet for the assignments you have today. If you don't have any work today, or are on a break from school, think about adding non-homework tasks. For example, you can estimate how long it will take to get ready in the morning, or how long it will take to clean your room. You can also experiment and guess how much time is spent on social media, games, etc., and then actually time yourself doing those things to see how close or far off your estimate was.

wORkSHeET:
Homework Organizer

_____
Date

Priority	Subject	Assignment	Due Date	Estimated Time	Actual Time	Completed

Copyright © 2019, Melissa Springstead Cahill. *ADHD in Teens & Young Adults*. All rights reserved.

MiNDfULnESs ExERcISe:
S.T.O.P.

Below is a mindfulness exercise that can be used at any time to help you slow down, calm your body and mind, and become curious about what you are experiencing. It is important to remind ourselves that the feelings, thoughts, and emotions we experience are *all* temporary.

It is an especially useful technique when you are starting homework or if you're feeling overwhelmed. In this chapter, it is natural to feel overwhelmed from the process of writing down and estimating the time spent on your homework, especially if you are stressed already. In cases like these:

S— Stop what you are doing

T— Take a few deep breaths. In through your nose, out through your mouth. Slowly. You can even do the 3-minute breathing meditation we have done already.

O— Observe what you are experiencing. What are you thinking and feeling? You can reflect on what you are noticing and also notice that thoughts are not facts. They are not permanent. Name the emotions you are feeling. Observe your body. How are you sitting? Any pain? Are you relaxed? What else?

P— Proceed with an open, curious, and *mindful* mind.

Copyright © 2019, Melissa Springstead Cahill. *ADHD in Teens & Young Adults*. All rights reserved.

ANCHOR IT!

- ***Mindfulness Meditation Tracking Sheet***
  - You can do the breathing exercises from Chapter 2, as well as those learned in this chapter: ***My World Around Me, Routine Activities***, and ***S.T.O.P***.

- ***Routine Activities:*** Remember to try to be mindful with whichever activity you decided to use. If you have a hard time remembering, try a different one!

- Fill out the ***Homework Organizer*** daily, as needed for homework (or other tasks if you don't have school or are on a break). Make sure to write down an estimated time before starting each assignment, and then use a stopwatch to time yourself.

Mindfulness Meditation Tracking Sheet

Week of: _____

DAY/DATE	DID YOU PRACTICE?	COMMENTS

Copyright © 2019, Melissa Springstead Cahill. *ADHD in Teens & Young Adults*. All rights reserved.

H: Happy Homework

LEARN IT!
- Overview of Homework as a Common Source of Stress
  - *My Stress Handout*

USE IT!
- Strategies for Tackling Homework and Schoolwork
  - *Long-Term Planner*
  - Does the Long-Term Planner Work?
- Importance of a Positive Mindset
  - *Positive Reflection*

ANCHOR IT!
- *Daily Gratitude Reflections*
- *Mindfulness Meditation Tracking Sheet*
- *Homework Organizer*
- *Long-Term Planner*

OVERVIEW OF HOMEWORK AS A COMMON SOURCE OF STRESS

If you're a teen, you're probably experiencing a decent amount of stress. Stress will make it hard to concentrate on day-to-day tasks, including homework. It's also very easy to get trapped in a cycle of negativity. For example, you may often feel stressed about the amount of homework you have, which, in turn, makes it difficult to complete that homework, which makes you even more stressed than you were before you started! Perhaps sometimes the stress has been so strong that you've attempted to avoid an assignment or had assignments that were past due. If so, did it create a situation later on that you felt was too big to fix? Have you ever sat down with a project that you knew was important to complete, but it was so big that you had no idea where to begin? Know that each of these situations are incredibly normal and common for young people with ADHD.

What's important in order to move forward is to create a foundation so that these situations become less common and occur less frequently. Perhaps one day, they won't occur at all. The goal in this chapter is to come face-to-face with your stress so that you can see it for what it is and develop a plan for dealing with it in a positive, constructive way. First, it is important to recognize the areas of your life that cause you stress in general so that you can try some things that will help reduce the impact that stress may have on you. In the following handout, list the things that bring the most stress to your life.

My Stress Handout

1. _____

2. _____

3. _____

4. _____

5. _____

6. _____

7. _____

8. _____

Which two of these things cause you the most stress?

_____

_____

_____

What has worked before to reduce the stress?

_____

_____

_____

Think of the things you have learned so far in this book (**Breathing Meditation, Weekly Schedule, Homework Organizer, Mindful Eating, S.T.O.P.**). Do you think that any of those will help with reducing your top two stressors? Can you think of other activities that may help?

_____

_____

_____

Copyright © 2019, Melissa Springstead Cahill. *ADHD in Teens & Young Adults*. All rights reserved.

STRATEGIES FOR TACKLING HOMEWORK AND SCHOOLWORK

Chapter 3 introduced the ***Homework Organizer*** as a tool for exercising your internal clock. As you performed the activities for that week, you may have noticed that your estimated time did not match your actual time, though of course it may have been more accurate for some subjects than for others. You also may have noticed that certain types of assignments, like writing a paper, took longer than others, like doing math problems. Or vice versa! This is an individualized experience, and there is no right or wrong.

You may have also noticed a difference when you had your phone in airplane mode vs. when notifications were allowed to freely come in. Often, that change makes a big difference in cutting down on homework time. When you prevent notifications from coming through, it is easier to focus and spend less (but more productive!) time on homework. It takes time for our internal clock to change, so keep doing this exercise until you notice that your estimated vs. actual times are closer together or the same.

When I introduced the ***Homework Organizer***, I recommended that you break longer assignments into smaller chunks. One reason for this is that it is common for adolescents (and even adults) to put things off and wait until the last minute—especially when it comes to bigger tasks or those that have a due date that is far in the future. This tendency to procrastinate results from an inability to keep track of time, as time management can be a difficult skill to master. However, if left unchecked, chronic procrastination and poor time management can lead to failure in school and interpersonal difficulties. **Metacognition**, which refers to the awareness you have of your own thought processes in general, helps to bring time into consciousness by helping you to slow down, pause, and reflect on what is happening. If you think about it, the ***S.T.O.P.*** method was intended to give you a metacognitive tool to regulate your emotions and slow things down when you need.

Even though they seem quite different, your work can be managed in a similar way to your emotions. By breaking a long-term project or assignment into daily tasks, it can help train your brain to see time differently, as well as to prevent that feeling of "last minute" cramming. When you have long-term tasks, the ***Long-Term Planner*** is an effective tool you can use to plan ahead and prevent procrastination. Although it is common to feel overwhelmed as you think about planning out a bigger task, once your plan is complete, you'll usually find that your stress and the degree to which you feel overwhelmed is significantly reduced.

How to use it:

- When you are assigned anything that takes longer than one or two days, use the ***Long-Term Planner*** to break down the task into manageable parts.
- Start by filling out the task, due date, and how many days you have to complete it.
- Then, fill out the day/dates where it says "Day 1, Day 2, etc."
- Next, record the due date in its appropriate column so you can see how many days you have to complete the task.
- Finally, think about how you would tackle the task. Which order would you work in? Do you need to organize your material first and then make a study guide? Do you already have a study guide, notes, etc.? If so, do you want to review and practice writing out what you know?

On the pages that follow are three examples of how to use the **_Long-Term Planner_**. These examples give you some ideas as to how you can use the planner for essays or tests. The first two sample planners cover a seven-day period, but they can be done for longer or shorter periods if needed. For example, the last sample planner, which spans 21 days, demonstrates how you might break down the process of studying for all your midterm or final exams.

SAMPLE LONG-TERM PLANNER #1:

History Test

Project / Test / Assignment: History Test About South America

Due Date: 3/17   Number of Days Before Due Date: 7

DAY 1 Saturday	DAY 2 Sunday	DAY 3 Monday	DAY 4 Tuesday	DAY 5 Wednesday	DAY 6 Thursday	DAY 7 Friday
Review	**Learn**	**Connect**	**Learn**	**Review**	**Summary**	**TEST**
Go over class discussions, notes, etc.

Organize all materials and homework

Combine all work into a study guide

**For example: typing an outline of the chapter and adding class material is a great way to get an overview of what you need to know | Make a table with key terms and definitions on the computer

Print out blank tables with only definitions and another table with only key terms

Test yourself by filling out the table by memory

Flashcards also work for some learners | Relate key terms back to parts of the chapter

Ask yourself: Why do I need to know this?

Why is this important?

What else do I know about this?

**Teaching the chapter out loud to someone else, or to yourself, is a great study tool | Learn map of South America

Find a blank map on the computer (Google images) or from your teacher

Print out a bunch of them and fill them out until you have 100% accuracy | Fill out a key terms table

Fill out blank map

Teach material to a friend, making connections between the map, key terms, and notes

Continue asking yourself questions to further your knowledge | Goal is to not have to learn any new material because you have already learned it throughout the week | |

Copyright © 2019, Melissa Springstead Cahill. *ADHD in Teens & Young Adults.* All rights reserved.

SAMPLE LONG-TERM PLANNER #2:

Essay/Paper

Project / Test / Assignment: _Essay/Paper_

Due Date: 4/14   Number of Days Before Due Date: 7

DAY 1 Saturday	DAY 2 Sunday	DAY 3 Monday	DAY 4 Tuesday	DAY 5 Wednesday	DAY 6 Thursday	DAY 7 Friday
Research/Thesis	**Outline**	**Draft**	**Break**	**Revision**	**Proofread**	**DUE**
Develop a thesis	Begin typing the outline. Fill in as much detail as you can with research. Do more research if needed	Turn the outline into a draft. Read through it to make sure that the paper flows nicely	If you have enough time, let your paper sit for a day. If not, then proofread and edit your paper	Check for: topic sentences, smooth transitions, intro and conclusion, support for your thesis	Read paper out loud and make corrections. Have someone else read your paper to make corrections	

Copyright © 2019, Melissa Springstead Cahill. *ADHD in Teens & Young Adults*. All rights reserved.

Long-Term Planner

Project / Test / Assignment: _____

Due Date: _____

Number of Days Before Due Date: _____

DAY 1 Saturday	DAY 2 Sunday	DAY 3 Monday	DAY 4 Tuesday	DAY 5 Wednesday	DAY 6 Thursday	DAY 7 Friday

Copyright © 2019, Melissa Springstead Cahill. *ADHD in Teens & Young Adults*. All rights reserved.

Sᴀᴍᴘʟᴇ Lᴏɴɢ-Tᴇʀᴍ Pʟᴀɴɴᴇʀ #3:
Final/Midterm Exam (Page 1)

Subject	Date of Tests	# of Days Before Tests	DAY 1 Saturday	DAY 2 Sunday	DAY 3 Monday	DAY 4 Tuesday	DAY 5 Wednesday	DAY 6 Thursday	DAY 7 Friday
Math			Organize material and write out study plan	Chapter 2		Chapter 3		Chapter 4 & 5	Chapter 6
English			Organize material and write out study plan	Vocab 1 (maybe quizlet?) Mark passages for essay	Vocab 2	Vocab 3 Meet with teacher to review passages	Vocab 4 Start outline	Vocab 5	Finish outline
Science			Organize material and write out study plan		Print all unit tests		Unit 1		Unit 2
History			Organize material and write out study plan	Print all unit tests	Terms Unit 1	Terms Unit 1	Terms Unit 2	Terms Unit 2	Terms Unit 3

Copyright © 2019, Melissa Springstead Cahill. *ADHD in Teens & Young Adults.* All rights reserved.

SaMpLe LoNG-TeRM PLANnER #3:
Final/Midterm Exam (Page 2)

Subject	Date of Tests	# of Days Before Tests	DAY 8 Saturday	DAY 9 Sunday	DAY 10 Monday	DAY 11 Tuesday	DAY 12 Wednesday	DAY 13 Thursday	DAY 14 Friday
Math			Chapter 7		Chapter 8	Practice problems from difficult sections	Practice problems from difficult sections	Practice problems from difficult sections	Review all
English			Vocab 1 & 2	Meet with teacher to review outline	Vocab 2 & 3		Vocab 4 & 5		All vocab
Science				Unit 3		Unit 4		Bubble maps or write-up of concepts to show connections	
History			Terms Unit 4	Terms Unit 4	Review old tests		Organize terms for possible essays	Organize terms for possible essays	Bubble maps or write-up of concepts to show connections

Copyright © 2019, Melissa Springstead Cahill. *ADHD in Teens & Young Adults*. All rights reserved.

SAMPLE LONG-TERM PLANNER #3:
Final/Midterm Exam (Page 3)

Subject	Date of Tests	# of Days Before Tests	DAY 15 Saturday	DAY 16 Sunday	DAY 17 Monday	DAY 18 Tuesday	DAY 19 Wednesday	DAY 20 Thursday	DAY 21 Friday
Math			Practice test	Review problem areas	No studying	FINAL			
English			Review all	Practice test – quizlet, vocab, practice essay	Review problem areas	No studying	FINAL		
Science			Teach someone (or talk out the concepts)	Review all	Practice test	Review problem areas	No studying	FINAL	
History			Teach someone (or talk out the concepts)		Review all	Practice test – possible bubble map or timeline off memory	Review problem areas	No studying	FINAL

Copyright © 2019, Melissa Springstead Cahill. *ADHD in Teens & Young Adults*. All rights reserved.

LONG-TERM PLANNER:
Final/Midterm Exam (Page 1)

Subject	Date of Tests	# of Days Before Tests	DAY 1 Saturday	DAY 2 Sunday	DAY 3 Monday	DAY 4 Tuesday	DAY 5 Wednesday	DAY 6 Thursday	DAY 7 Friday

Copyright © 2019, Melissa Springstead Cahill. *ADHD in Teens & Young Adults*. All rights reserved.

Long-Term Planner:
Final/Midterm Exam (Page 2)

Subject	Date of Tests	# of Days Before Tests	DAY 8 Saturday	DAY 8 Sunday	DAY 10 Monday	DAY 11 Tuesday	DAY 12 Wednesday	DAY 13 Thursday	DAY 14 Friday

Copyright © 2019, Melissa Springstead Cahill. *ADHD in Teens & Young Adults*. All rights reserved.

LONG-TERM PLANNER:
Final/Midterm Exam (Page 3)

Subject	Date of Tests	# of Days Before Tests	DAY 15 Saturday	DAY 16 Sunday	DAY 17 Monday	DAY 18 Tuesday	DAY 19 Wednesday	DAY 20 Thursday	DAY 21 Friday

Copyright © 2019, Melissa Springstead Cahill. *ADHD in Teens & Young Adults*. All rights reserved.

Now that you have seen these examples, think about if you have anything coming up that would benefit from using the ***Long-Term Planner***. If so, go ahead and try filling it out now. When using the planner for the first time, it can help if you brainstorm before filling the days out.

TIP: Whenever you use the Long-Term Planner, make sure to write the daily tasks onto the Homework Organizer.

CaSE StUDy – Does the Long-Term Planner Really Work?

Sometimes students are intimidated to try a new system. I wanted to share with you a story I received from a former client of mine, who once stood exactly where you are now. Hearing her experience with the planner and how she integrated it into her life (as well as the benefits she found by doing so) can be valuable in reducing some of the anxiety in taking that first step. She writes:

"In high school, I had a major problem with time management. Luckily, procrastination was not my issue but, rather, how to strategically conquer imminent deadlines for a large final project or major exam. The complexity and work required to complete these tasks would loom over my head and exacerbate my anxiety to the point that the quality of work diminished. Assignments and tests began to take over and led to negative spillover effects in other facets of my life: extracurricular activities, social life, and, most of all, mental health.

Melissa introduced me to two ingenious planning techniques: the homework organizer and the long-term planner. The homework organizer went a step beyond a typical store-bought planner because it had a column labeled 'Time,' encouraging me to make an estimate for how long a certain assignment or studying session should take. This worked well for me in two ways. First, it held me accountable for focusing on an assignment by trying to stick within my designated time parameters so that I was better engaged with the material, retaining more information, and increasing my efficiency. The benefit to this was that it also instilled a sense of work-life balance I needed because I was adhering to a time limit and then closing my books so that I could remind myself when to stop. I remember Melissa telling me how difficult it is to know when you know material for an exam, so having a time limit could help me mitigate cramming or over studying, both of which I had done prior to using this new homework organizer.

The long-term planner helped immensely with planning out strategies to complete large projects and exams. The general idea behind it is that I mapped out the number of days until the assignment due date or exam day, and then I filled in what I needed to do every day to complete the task bit-by-bit rather than all at once. This worked again to both lower anxiety levels propagated from a 'looming' feeling and also made me engage with study skills. Instead of just opening up my notes or textbook to start trying to mindlessly digest information, I began to group information thematically since I was writing down units as a checklist I needed to study on a given day rather than grouping it all together.

The two planning techniques were vital to my success in high school and continue to play a major role in my achievement in college. I am now able to breakdown assignments to lessen their 'Goliath' presence and methodically think through study strategies to best determine how I can engage with material and tackle tasks in intervals."

– E.G., 21

Hopefully, this testimonial will make placing your trust and commitment in this powerful tool just a little bit easier, and, like E.G., you may be surprised to find what a difference it makes once you begin to incorporate it into your daily set of activities as a student.

THE IMPORTANCE OF A POSITIVE MINDSET

Across school, home, and social demands, it is common for all of us to experience stress in some form or another. You have already learned some ways to reduce stress, and here I will introduce you to another tool that can help in this regard: keeping a positive mindset. Focusing on the positive aspects of your life helps you to balance out the negative, more stressful aspects, which, in turn, helps to calm your body and mind. Happiness comes from inside us, so it's important to reflect on what we recognize is going great in our lives as well.

wORkSHeET:
Positive Reflection

Think about something in your life that is positive and you are grateful for. It could be a tangible thing, like a person, or it could be a memory. **Write down below what you are thinking about.**

_____

_____

_____

_____

Write more about what this means to you and why.

_____

_____

_____

_____

Does this thing know that it is important to you? If so, how? If not, should it?

_____

_____

_____

_____

Copyright © 2019, Melissa Springstead Cahill. *ADHD in Teens & Young Adults*. All rights reserved.

Over the next week, reflect and pay attention to good things that happen throughout your day. Before bed, you can use a journal to write down some things that you are grateful for. You can also start your day by thinking about your schedule and intentions for the day and reflect on the positive day or week ahead of you. If you find that there are things that are causing stress, remind yourself that these feelings and thoughts are temporary. You can also then see if you can change the wording of your thoughts to be more positive. For example, if you have a role in a school play, try focusing on the positive aspects of that day. Rather than getting caught up in thoughts like, "I'm not sure if I will have my lines memorized," try reminding yourself that "It will be good to have my grandparents in the crowd to see my performance." Or, if you have a big school project that is making you nervous, you might say to yourself, "I was stressed this time last year, and the final project actually turned out to be a great opportunity to raise my grade." Similarly, if you are studying for a test but not completely prepared yet, you might say, "It feels great to know that I have 80% of my notes done already."

Consider putting a reminder in your phone to help create the habit of reflecting on the positive and being grateful. At the end of this chapter is a template called ***Daily Gratitude Reflections*** that you can follow for writing down things that you are grateful for.

CASE STUDY – From Teens Like You!

"In my first year of high school, I was so angry. I was going to a school with a lot of rich kids who always seemed to have the things I wanted but couldn't have. I didn't get along with my teachers. I had just moved into the area, and I also didn't have any friends. My parents didn't understand, and we would fight because they felt I was ungrateful.

I started having a hard time falling asleep because my mind would just race with negative thoughts. I felt that people wouldn't want to make friends with the poor, stupid kid, and my life was going to be hard forever. I would flip flop between feeling angry and hurt.

When Melissa first had me do the daily gratitude reflections, I thought it was going to be a dumb idea. However, I started to learn how I was looking at everything around me in what Melissa called 'absolutes.' For example, I thought that EVERYONE had it easy, I had NOTHING, that EVERYTHING was wrong, or that NOBODY cared about me. Being mindful about my life helped me to have a better idea of what I looked forward to and what actually made me happy. It let me see the things about school that I actually liked. Or days when I did have good luck.

Now I try to end my day by thinking about something positive that happened. It sounds simple, but really focusing on this has helped me sleep better and wake up the next morning with a positive attitude. I am also closer with my parents because I can see how hard they try to provide me with a great life. Now I have a lot of good friends.

Being positive is a choice you can make. I learned that sometimes you need to have someone help you see how to make that choice. To a kid my age, I would say try the gratitude exercise with your whole heart and see if it helps your whole life."

– S.B., 14

ANCHOR IT!

- *Mindfulness Meditation Tracking Sheet*

- *Homework Organizer* and *Long-Term Planner* (connecting to your *Weekly Schedule*)

- *Daily Gratitude Reflections*

wORkSHeET:
Daily Gratitude Reflections

I am grateful for...

1. _____
2. _____
3. _____

3 amazing things that happened today were...

1. _____
2. _____
3. _____

I can do these 3 things tomorrow to make it great...

1. _____
2. _____
3. _____

Copyright © 2019, Melissa Springstead Cahill. *ADHD in Teens & Young Adults*. All rights reserved.

Mindfulness Meditation Tracking Sheet

Week of: _____

DAY/DATE	DID YOU PRACTICE?	COMMENTS

Copyright © 2019, Melissa Springstead Cahill. *ADHD in Teens & Young Adults*. All rights reserved.

CHAPTER 5

O: Open and Organized

LEARN IT!

- The importance of being open to new techniques and systems for how you organize yourself and for how you study.

USE IT!

- Backpack and Study Space Cleanout
  - Mindfully Cleaning and Organizing Your Backpack
  - "Where Does This Paper Go?"
  - Organizing Your Study Space
- Study Strategies: What Kind of Learner Are You?
  - *CITE Learning Styles Instrument*
    - *Study Techniques and Ideas*
    - *A New Study Technique*
    - Meditation: *Test-Taking Guided Meditation*

ANCHOR IT!

- *Organizing Your Study Space*
- *A New Study Technique*
- *Test-Taking Guided Meditation Script*
- *Mindfulness Meditation Tracking Sheet*

BEING OPEN TO NEW STRATEGIES FOR STUDYING AND ORGANIZING

Do you remember when you were in elementary school and your teachers would tell you how to study for tests? Some common strategies that teachers often recommend in early elementary school are the use of flashcards, worksheets, study guides, re-reading chapters, memorizing facts, and making mind-maps. You may also remember that in early elementary school, you were taught a particular style of organizing your schoolwork. Teachers would often tell you exactly what school supplies you needed and how to set it all up. For example, you may have had a third grade teacher who wanted you to have all subjects in a binder with a specific way of using dividers. Then, in fourth grade, your teacher wanted everything separate and for you to use spiral notebooks.

As you have gotten older, and as the material has become more complex, you may find that the strategies you used before no longer work as well. It is important to recognize that in your early days of learning, teachers presented a variety of strategies to lay the foundation for all types of learners. However, if you find that those strategies are no longer working, then it may be time to investigate whether or not you are studying and organizing for your learning style. In this chapter, we will explore various learning styles and give you other strategies to try using. Hopefully, you are at a place where your teachers will allow you to experiment with and integrate these approaches into your own work in a way that is still respectful of their class expectations.

BACKPACK AND STUDY SPACE CLEANOUT

Before we get to the organization of your actual school supplies, we need to take a look at what is in your backpack and study area. Having a calm, clean, minimally cluttered, and organized study space and backpack can help both your mind and levels of productivity. A lot of people feel anxious and unfocused when things are out of order. It can also lead to stress with parents, caregivers, or teachers. Your parent may ask you to grab something quickly to get out of the house on time, but you can't find it, and they may become upset with you. Or, imagine that your teacher asks you and your classmates to turn in your homework. You know you did it, but you can't find it—which, of course, leaves the teacher thinking that you didn't actually complete it. These situations are only a couple of examples of incidents that can occur when your backpack and study space are cluttered and disorganized.

Can you think of some examples when your space being disorganized led to stress because you misplaced or lost something? If so, how did you feel? Where you frustrated, annoyed, angry? If not, reflect on what you have done to create a space that eliminates the stress that comes with misplacing or losing something.

In addition to causing you to misplace and/or lose things, having too much physical clutter can lead to internal or mental clutter, which makes it difficult to think and act. When there is too much competing visual stimuli, the brain becomes distracted as it tries to decide what to focus on. However, this does not mean that your space needs to be "perfect." Rather, it means that the space you spend the most time in should be organized in a way that makes it easy to find what you need. Often, having a more organized space can relieve the anxiety and stress of misplacing or losing things.

Although we are only addressing your backpack and study space, you can also think about spending some time cleaning and organizing your other spaces (such as the bedroom or family room). When you start each day with a more organized space, you'll find that it's surprisingly easy to maintain if you have the right mindset. One way to try and keep your space organized is by using a **"one touch" rule**, where all things are only touched once to get them to their "home." For example, when you get home, you take your shoes off. Instead of leaving them in the middle of the floor, you touch them once and put them in your closet (or wherever they belong). This approach can help you to make sure that things don't pile up, or when they do, that there isn't nearly as much that needs to be done in order to re-organize.

TIP: A great guideline to follow: "Only touch things once!"

Mindfully Cleaning and Organizing Your Backpack

We are going to start the process of organizing by focusing on a space that is small, but very important: your backpack or school bag. If possible, try to do this near the space that you typically study, as well as near a trash can (or get a trash bag). Our goal is to help everything have a home, or space where that object belongs without you having to think too much about it. Let's start by opening up your backpack. Before pulling anything out, notice what it looks like.

> *Is it neat?*
>
> *Does it look organized?*
>
> *Is it messy or overstuffed?*

What feelings come up for you when you look at it? Are you wanting to avoid doing this exercise, or are you excited to get more space or have a better system? Alternately, does it feel like your backpack doesn't need organizing? Regardless of your answers, try to keep an open mind to see if any changes in this space might make any other areas of your life easier.

1. Empty out each pocket. Once you think all items are removed, turn your backpack upside down and shake it to make sure nothing is still in there (you may want to do this over a trash can in case you have pencil shavings, trash, etc.). Throw all trash away as you take it out of the backpack.

2. Separate the loose papers and put them in a stack. If you have binders or spiral notebooks, make sure to take out any loose paper from there as well.

3. Take a look at your binders. Are they organized and separated by subject or by parts of class? For example, if your binder has all core subject classes, does it have a clear separation of where one class ends and another one starts? Within a subject, are things separated clearly (e.g., do you have homework, notes, graded work, etc., labeled clearly)?

4. Do you have any spiral notebooks? If so, are they separated by class, or do you use them for everything and have multiple subjects in each one?

If your binder and notebooks are disorganized…

- Get dividers and use them to separate each subject, as well as different sections or obligations within each class. For example, the dividers could be for:
    - Homework
    - Notes
    - Graded work
    - Labs (if a science class)
    - Any others
- Should you separate the binder and have a small divider for each subject?
- Notebook: Do you have multiple notebooks, or just one per class? If it seems that you are combining subjects, then consider getting one larger notebook for multiple subjects.

Once you have an idea of your organization system (binders vs. notebooks), we are going to see where your loose papers can go. If some are definitely trash and you're sure they are no longer useful, then go ahead and throw them out now. Even if you were already tested on the materials, make sure that you keep anything that could help you study for a midterm or final exam (or future courses that build on each other).

Some things to think about with regard to loose papers: Did you find any papers that you have been (or were) looking for? Teachers often pass things out at the end of class, which leads students to stuff those papers into their backpacks. Does that happen to you? Do you think that one of the papers you found in your backpack was misplaced or loose in a random place for another reason? We want to make sure that these papers have homes so that you do not lose anything in the future, as that would lead to unnecessary stress. If you found that many of the loose papers were homework assignments, things that needed to be given to your parents, or things that needed to go back to school/teacher, it may be helpful to have a designated homework folder. This folder can be used specifically for the loose papers that normally would be put into random parts of your backpack. Label one side "To Do" and the other side "Turn In."

"Where Does This Paper Go?"

While you are organizing the papers in your backpack, it is incredibly important to consider each of the following questions:

- Do I need this again? If not, put it in the trash or recycling bin.
- Is this something for my parent/caregiver? If so, give it to them.
- Is this specific to a class? If yes, put it in that binder/folder.
- Does this paper have a date that I need to know? If so, put it on the calendar, and then recycle it.
- Does this need to be turned in to a teacher? If so, put it in your homework folder in the "Turn In" section.
- Is this something I am still working on? If yes, put it in your homework folder in the "To Do" section.

CASE STUDY – From Teens Like You!

"My backpack used to be a mess. Papers were loose everywhere, and I had books and pencils and note cards and folders just shoved in anywhere they could go. My grades were bad because of missing work. I would talk to my teacher and tell her that I did a lot of the assignments, but I could tell that she and my parents thought I was lying. I would sometimes find missing assignments at the bottom of my backpack, but it was months after they were due, so I could not get any points from it.

I didn't want to organize my backpack because it seemed like a lot of work and because I felt like I could usually find what I was looking for. But when Melissa had me actually do it, it really only took about 20 minutes. I promised I would try to keep things organized.

That next week I saved a lot more than 20 minutes. I knew where to look for everything, where every paper went, and where my assignments were written down so I could get started faster. But I also noticed that I didn't procrastinate as much because of anxiety of not knowing where something was. Now I keep my backpack really organized. It's easy when you make a place for everything to go! But I learned that you have to start somewhere."

– A.G., 13

Organizing Your Study Space

Do you have a designated study space, or do you decide where to do homework on a day-to-day basis? If you decide that you do rotate between where you study, consider organizing the most common space you use. It is very common for a person's study space to become full of clutter and become a home for "lost" papers. Some students rotate from space to space simply because they don't have a clear or effectively organized area where they can do work. If this is the case for you, then taking the time to organize a certain study area can help you have a designated study space in the future!

Once you have decided where to organize, sit down and take a look around the space. What do you see? Is it calming, chaotic, or overwhelming? Do you see a random knick-knack that you got years ago and did not notice until now? Do you see trash? If there are drawers, are they full or empty? Realize that it is normal to feel overwhelmed when reflecting on your space. Make sure to breathe and remind yourself that the feeling you are experiencing is temporary and will pass. It may also be helpful to get a parent/caregiver to help you with this exercise. Come up with a plan of how much needs to be organized. If you know that this will become a large project that you may not have time to do now, then you may want to schedule it for a later date.

When creating an organized, effective study space, it is important to remember that the goal isn't simply to get rid of everything! A *bare* desk isn't necessarily an effective one. Rather, the goal is to have a desk that makes it easier for you to complete tasks without losing anything. For example, you might want to organize your desk so that you have a basket of your favorite pens and pencils within easy reach. Stacking trays make it easy to give assignments that have been returned to you a place to go. A dry erase board or a calendar over your desk gives you a central place to record incoming assignments and important due dates, and it ensures that you're on track with your workload. Drawer dividers can separate things like paper clips, scissors, tape, and colored pencils so that everything has a home without seeming like "a drawer full of random stuff." It is also important to remember that visual clutter can make it harder for the brain to stay focused, so if you have a lot of extra knick-knacks, consider moving them to an area that is not in your study space.

At the very end of this chapter, you'll find a shopping list that will help you take the first steps into organizing your schoolwork. For example, you'll find binders and dividers among the bullet points. However, feel free to add to the bullet points that are already there! Think about what might help you create locations that are easy to search, easy to work with, and help provide stability throughout your day.

STUDY STRATEGIES: WHAT KIND OF LEARNER ARE YOU?

The idea that the study strategies you successfully used before are no longer working—given that you are now learning more complex material—was introduced earlier in this chapter. Adolescents often consider *time* when thinking about how prepared they are, and parents will also often say that their child needs to spend more *time* studying. Instead, it may be more helpful to consider the *way* you study vs. the amount of time you study.

Consider this: When you study in a way that is not best for your learning style, you might work for hours and hours and still not get results. However, when studying the same material using a strategy that works for you, you may find that you can spend less time and get more accurate or consistent results. There are a lot of ways to determine how you learn. There are online learning quizzes that may be fun to take and can teach you what your preference is. Make sure to be curious about the results and look at them as a potential preference, not as an absolute learning style. The **CITE Learning Styles Instrument** (CITE; Babich, Burdine, Albright, & Randol, 1976) is a test often used by teachers to help them determine the preferred learning styles of their students. While you are not doing the activity for the benefit of your teacher, you may find it very useful in showing how you gather information, what your best work conditions are, and how you express the knowledge you have. For example, here are a few of the CITE components:

- **Information Gathering**: What data do you process best? Audio, numerical, or visual?
- **Work Conditions**: Do you work best alone or with a group?
- **Expressiveness**: Do you best express yourself through oral or written communication?

CITE summarizes the type of learner a student is within the following areas: visual-language, visual-numerical, auditory-language, auditory-numerical, auditory-visual-kinesthetic, social-individual, social-group, expressiveness-oral, and expressiveness-written. The learning styles are then categorized as major, minor, or negligible. If you already know your learning style, then skip the inventory and move to the next section. If you are curious about what type of learner you may be, then consider doing the following CITE Inventory.

wORkSHeET:
CITE Learning Styles Instrument

Answer all the questions. There are no right or wrong answers.

		Most Like Me		Least Like Me	
1.	When I make things for my studies, I remember what I have learned better.	4	3	2	1
2.	Written assignments are easy for me to do.	4	3	2	1
3.	I learn better if someone reads a book to me than if I read silently to myself.	4	3	2	1
4.	I learn best when I study alone.	4	3	2	1
5.	Having assignment directions on the board makes them easier to understand.	4	3	2	1
6.	It's harder for me to do a written assignment than an oral one.	4	3	2	1
7.	When I do math problems in my head, I say the numbers to myself.	4	3	2	1
8.	If I need help in the subject, I will ask a classmate for help.	4	3	2	1
9.	I understand a math problem that is written down better than one I hear.	4	3	2	1
10.	I don't mind doing written assignments.	4	3	2	1
11.	Written assignments are easy for me to do.	4	3	2	1
12.	I remember more of what learn if I learn it when I am alone.	4	3	2	1
13.	I would rather read a story than listen to it read.	4	3	2	1
14.	I feel like I talk smarter than I write.	4	3	2	1
15.	If someone tells me three numbers to add, I can usually get the right answer without writing them down.	4	3	2	1
16.	I like to work in a group because I learn from the others in my group.	4	3	2	1
17.	Written math problems are easier for me to do than oral ones.	4	3	2	1
18.	Writing a spelling word several times helps me remember it better.	4	3	2	1
19.	I find it easier to remember what I have heard than what I have read.	4	3	2	1
20.	It is more fun to learn with classmates at first, but it is hard to study with them.	4	3	2	1
21.	I like written directions better than spoken ones.	4	3	2	1

Copyright © 2019, Melissa Springstead Cahill. *ADHD in Teens & Young Adults*. All rights reserved.

	Most Like Me		Least Like Me	
22. If homework were oral, I would do it all.	4	3	2	1
23. When I hear a phone number, I can remember it without writing it down.	4	3	2	1
24. I get more work done when I work with someone else.	4	3	2	1
25. Seeing a number makes more sense to me than hearing a number.	4	3	2	1
26. I like to do things like simple repairs or crafts with my hands.	4	3	2	1
27. The things I write on paper sound better than when I say them.	4	3	2	1
28. I study best when there is no one around to talk or listen to.	4	3	2	1
29. I would rather read things in a book than have the teacher tell me about them.	4	3	2	1
30. Speaking is a better way than writing if you want someone to understand it better.	4	3	2	1
31. When I have written a math problem to do, I say it to myself to understand it better.	4	3	2	1
32. I can learn more about a subject if I am with a small group of students.	4	3	2	1
33. Seeing the price of something written down is easier for me to understand than having someone tell me the price.	4	3	2	1
34. I like to make things with my hands.	4	3	2	1
35. I like tests that call for sentence completion or written answers.	4	3	2	1
36. I understand more from a class discussion than from reading about the subject.	4	3	2	1
37. I remember the spelling of a word better if I see it written down than if someone spells it out loud.	4	3	2	1
38. Spelling and grammar rules make it hard for me to say what I want in writing.	4	3	2	1
39. It makes it easier when I say the numbers of a problem to myself as I work it out.	4	3	2	1
40. I like to study with other people.	4	3	2	1
41. When teachers say a number, I really don't understand it until I see it written down.	4	3	2	1
42. I understand what I have learned well when I am involved in making something for the subject.	4	3	2	1
43. Sometimes I say dumb things, but writing gives me time to correct myself.	4	3	2	1
44. I do well on tests if they are about things I hear in class.	4	3	2	1
45. I can't think as well when I work with someone else as when I work alone.	4	3	2	1

Copyright © 2019, Melissa Springstead Cahill. *ADHD in Teens & Young Adults*. All rights reserved.

Below is the scoring sheet to determine your learning style. Write the number you circled for each question in terms of whether it is "most like" or "least like" you. Then, add each column and multiply the total by 2.

Visual-Language

5 _____
13 _____
21 _____
29 _____
37 _____
Total _____ × 2 = _____

Visual-Numerical

9 _____
17 _____
25 _____
33 _____
41 _____
Total _____ × 2 = _____

Social-Individual

4 _____
12 _____
20 _____
28 _____
45 _____
Total _____ × 2 = _____

Social-Group

8 _____
16 _____
24 _____
32 _____
40 _____
Total _____ × 2 = _____

Auditory-Language

3 _____
11 _____
19 _____
36 _____
44 _____
Total _____ × 2 = _____

Auditory-Numerical

7 _____
15 _____
23 _____
31 _____
39 _____
Total _____ × 2 = _____

Expressiveness-Oral

6 _____
14 _____
22 _____
30 _____
38 _____
Total _____ × 2 = _____

Expressiveness-Written

2 _____
10 _____
27 _____
35 _____
43 _____
Total _____ × 2 = _____

Kinesthetic-Tactile

1 _____
18 _____
26 _____
34 _____
42 _____
Total _____ × 2 = _____

Score: 33 – 40 = Major Learning Style
20 – 32 = Minor Learning Style
5 – 20 = Negligible Use

Put a star next to or circle your major learning style(s). You can have more than one. On the page that follows is a list of learning styles with definitions and techniques to try. Highlight, star, or mark up the styles that you scored highest on. You should have one for Language, Numerical, Social, and Expressiveness.

Copyright © 2019, Melissa Springstead Cahill. *ADHD in Teens & Young Adults.* All rights reserved.

KEY: Study Techniques and Ideas

Learning Style	Definition	Study Techniques
Visual-Language	- Learn well from seeing words - Remember more when reading or watching - Fast thinker	- Write down notes so that you can read them and study from them - Make practice tests that you can take rather than being quizzed orally
Visual-Numerical	- Need to see numbers on the board or written down - Not good at doing problems in your head - Fast thinker	- See all numbers written down - Show all your work to prevent careless mistakes
Auditory-Language	- Learn from hearing words - May have difficulty taking notes	- Record information and re-listen to it - Use audio books (audible.com)
Auditory-Numerical	- Learn from hearing numbers - Able to work problems in your head - May have difficulty taking notes	- Teach others math concepts - Record explanations and listen to them while studying
Kinesthetic	- Learn best by doing and moving - Seek out feeling and touch - Sensitive to others' feelings - Good at applying what is learned to real-life situations	- Engage in physical movement while learning - Doodle *(only if it doesn't distract you)* - Apply things being learned to real-life situations
Social-Individual	- Get more work done alone - Prefer to study alone	- Don't do group work when given an option
Social-Group	- Like to study with others - Like others' ideas to help them learn	- Learn with one other person - Be careful about number of people - Make sure to not work with friends who may prevent you from working
Expressiveness-Oral	- Able to tell you what they know - Sometimes know more than what the test shows - Have difficulty putting thoughts on paper	- Choose oral reports when given an option
Expressiveness-Written	- Good at writing essays - Feel more comfortable giving written answers rather than oral - Thoughts are better organized on paper	- Write reports - Write out notes - Write out information while studying

Copyright © 2019, Melissa Springstead Cahill. *ADHD in Teens & Young Adults*. All rights reserved.

A New Study Technique

What are my Major Learning Styles?

Numerical: _____ **Language:** _____

Expressiveness: _____ **Social:** _____

Kinesthetic: Yes _____ or No _____

What are some new study techniques I could try based on my learning style?

_____

_____

_____

Which one will I use over the next week?

_____

_____

_____

Reflect on the experience: Did I like it? Did it help, and how do I know?

_____

_____

_____

Copyright © 2019, Melissa Springstead Cahill. *ADHD in Teens & Young Adults.* All rights reserved.

CASE STUDY – From Teens Like You!

"I remember that seventh grade was the first year I thought was really hard. For almost all of junior high school and high school I hated the day that report cards would come out because I knew I would have the same fight with my parents. They would tell me things like, 'Why don't you try harder?' or 'Aren't you listening when the teacher is talking?' It felt like everyone got school but me.

By ninth grade I was spending HOURS doing my homework, but I still felt like I was barely getting a C average. I felt like I was stupid. I couldn't remember anything from class, even though I was there the whole time. It seemed like it took me an entire night to do something that took a classmate only a few minutes. I felt like I was being irresponsible or lazy if I did anything for myself.

When Melissa had me do the CITE, it helped me to see that I wasn't stupid. I just never learned how to learn in a way that worked for me. Experimenting with the way I did homework showed me it wasn't just about the time I spent studying, but how I was able to keep things in my brain. It also helped me to see how certain things worked or didn't work for me based on my ADD.

Now I use a lot of visual tools like a white board and online flash cards. I watch more videos about subjects that are hard for me, and then I can explain them in my own words. My grades are much better than before, and I spend way less time on homework!"

– C.M., 15

Test-Taking Guided Meditation

Test-taking is something that just about everyone feels anxious about. It is extremely frustrating when you study, know the material, and then your mind goes blank when you sit down to take the test. This typically happens when the brain locks up due to stress and anxiety. When this happens, it is nearly impossible to access the material stored until the body and mind have calmed down.

One way to prevent test anxiety is to visualize yourself taking a test, answering questions correctly, and feeling relaxed. In doing so, you are tricking your mind into going to a positive place, instead of allowing it to generate a laundry list of things that could go wrong in a worst-case scenario. Therefore, whenever you feel anxiety creeping in and find yourself thinking pessimistically about how a test will go, try to picture a best-case scenario. Remember times when you were stressed out going into a previous test, only to look over the material and say to yourself, "Hey—this isn't so bad!" Remember times when you felt confident answering a block of questions and how the pen seemed to move on its own as you wrote down everything you knew.

Keep in mind that some level of anxiety can be useful for human beings when they are about to encounter a future checkpoint. For example, if you're worried that a test will be hard because you still don't know an entire chapter of material, you've identified a problem that needs to be solved. Rather than simply getting stuck in this worry, use your anxiety as a means by which to take initiative. What are ways that you can become an expert in the material before the test arrives? Is there a study guide that exists? Can you meet with a friend to talk through the tough stuff? Once you've put in the time and effort to solve the problems you anticipate in advance of the test, it will be easier to picture yourself working steadily and confidently on test day.

Of course, it may very well be that you still feel anxious even after you've done all the prep work that it seems you can do. Here is where mindfulness can be a tremendous asset! If you can reasonably say to yourself, "I've done as much as any person could do to prepare for this test," then you know that any lingering anxiety and associated negative beliefs are simply intrusive thoughts that can be treated accordingly. At this point, you can begin using the ***Test-Taking Guided Meditation*** to help you feel good about what you've accomplished and visualize those efforts leading to future success. I suggest consulting the script whenever you find that anxious thoughts are beginning to intrude. However, if you have always struggled with test anxiety, then try performing the meditation three times a week *even if* you don't have any upcoming tests. Doing so will help re-train your mind and body from going to a negative emotional place whenever an academic challenge arises.

ANCHOR IT!

- ***Mindfulness Meditation Tracking Sheet***

- Continue-cleaning and organizing study space: desk, room etc.

- Use a ***New Study Technique*** and reflect on the experience.

- Listen to the ***Test-Taking Guided Meditation*** to mentally prepare for an upcoming test. If there are no tests this week, then use the meditation with anything else that may be stressful or anxiety-provoking.

Possible Shopping List:

- Binder
- Dividers
- Notebook(s): One multi-subject notebook or multiple smaller ones
- Folder
- Sheet protectors: Buy the less durable ones in bulk. This way, you have them whenever needed.

MiNDfULnESs ExERcISe:
Test-Taking Guided Meditation Script

Sit comfortably with your feet on the ground and your eyes closed. You may rest your hands wherever they feel comfortable. Imagine that it is the morning before a test and you have just arrived at school. As you walk onto campus, you see your friends and classmates. You may even see your teacher.

During this time, your mind and body are relaxed. Even though you notice that a few of the students around you are nervous, you feel confident that you did your best to prepare and are ready to take the test. As you get closer to the classroom, you notice your heart starting to beat a little faster.

You acknowledge the feeling and remind yourself that you are prepared and ready to take this test.

You are now inside the classroom and seated at your desk. You are prepared and ready to take this test.

As the test is passed out, you are calm, focused, and ready to begin. The test has now started. You are answering each question thoroughly and slowly. You are reading all directions to all problems completely and answering with confidence.

Every question you get to is familiar. You have studied and learned the concepts and ideas being asked in the questions. You continue until the test is complete.

You then turn the test in to the teacher and return to your seat. You feel happy that the test is over and accomplished, knowing that your hard work paid off. Enjoy this moment of reflection in knowing you did the best you could.

When you hear the bell, you may open your eyes and return to the room.

Copyright © 2019, Melissa Springstead Cahill. *ADHD in Teens & Young Adults*. All rights reserved.

Mindfulness Meditation Tracking Sheet

Week of: _____

DAY/DATE	DID YOU PRACTICE?	COMMENTS

Copyright © 2019, Melissa Springstead Cahill. *ADHD in Teens & Young Adults*. All rights reserved.

CHApTER 6

R: Recognize, Relax, and Reflect

LEARN IT!

- The 3 R's

USE IT!

- Mindfulness Exercises:
    - *Focusing on the Five Senses*
    - *Counting to 100*
    - *4-7-8 Breathing*
    - *Body Scan Meditation*
- Multitasking
    - *Multitasking*
    - *Reflections on Monotasking vs. Multitasking*
- Setting Intentions
    - *Seeing My Future*

ANCHOR IT!

- *4-7-8 Breathing Method*
- *No Multitasking*
- *Body Scan Meditation*
- *Mindfulness Meditation Tracking Sheet*

THE 3 R'S: RECOGNIZE, RELAX, AND REFLECT

In our busy lives, we deal with all kinds of academic and social pressures. It is common for our stress to be high! It is important to **Recognize** when we may need to use a strategy to cope with this reality. By using different strategies, we may find that our body and mind are more able to **Relax**, allowing for **Reflection** to happen. By being curious about our experiences while using the interventions and strategies mentioned in this book, you are allowing yourself to really master what works for you. The more mindfulness exercises that you have in your toolkit, the more likely you are to help calm your body and mind, leading to more fulfilled and happy lives. Each of the following exercises are ones that you can experiment with over the next week.

FOCUSING ON THE FIVE SENSES

Paying attention to your senses (e.g., vision, hearing, taste, smell, touch) is a great way to be mindful and reconnect to the present moment. For example, take a deep breath right now through your nose. What do you smell? Can you pinpoint where those aromas might be coming from? Now, pay attention to the sounds in the room. What are all of the different, distinct sounds that you hear? At night, you might be aware of the sounds of crickets, the hum of a fan, the clicking of a nearby clock, or a dog barking outside.

How is this useful? When we recognize that we are in a more stressed state, we can focus on engaging our senses—one at a time—in order to help our body and mind calm down. By isolating each sense, it is like you are casting out an anchor that helps you to slow down and gives your brain a break from worrying, to-do lists, pressures, etc. Although we do constantly engage our senses throughout our day-to-day lives, we typically do so all at the same time. **In contrast, engaging each sense independently reminds us that we have more control over what we experience than we realize, and we can give certain sensations a higher or lower priority than others. This next exercise focuses on engaging and connecting with each sense independently.**

wORkSHeET:
Focusing on the Five Senses

Sit with your hands folded in your lap, or another similarly comfortable position. There is no need to set a timer or meditation bell. While you'll want to focus on each sense for about two to three minutes, you don't need to keep count or monitor the time exactly. Be present in the moment, and start by taking a few deep belly breaths.

Sense of <u>VISION</u>: What catches your visual attention? Is it colorful? What is its shape?

1.

2.

3.

Sense of <u>HEARING</u>: What do you hear? Is it something specific? Is it a sound within your body?

1.

2.

3.

Sense of <u>TASTE</u>: Do you taste anything in your mouth? Is it neutral? Sweet? Bitter?

1.

2.

3.

Sense of <u>SMELL</u>: Do you smell something specific, or is it neutral?

1.

2.

3.

Sense of <u>TOUCH</u>: What are you in contact with? Is it tangible (like a couch) or something intangible (like the wind or temperature)?

1.

2.

3.

Copyright © 2019, Melissa Springstead Cahill. *ADHD in Teens & Young Adults*. All rights reserved.

Now that you have spent some time engaging your senses while doing the previous exercise, take five minutes and move to another area. If you are inside, maybe go outside. If that is not possible, then consider going to another area of your house. If you are in your room, maybe go to the kitchen or living room. Set a timer for five minutes total, and when you are ready, take a deep breath and focus on each sense slowly and mindfully.

Feel free to spend more time on one sense over another if you feel like it. Feel and become curious about the sensations and feelings that are present. If you see something that starts to remind you of something else (e.g., noticing that a house across the street might look like your grandmother's, and remembering a time from your childhood), then acknowledge that thought and try to let go of it without getting stuck in it. Instead, focus back on the experience whenever you notice your mind starting to wander.

Did you notice anything different doing this a second time? Was the experience the same or different?

_____

_____

_____

Copyright © 2019, Melissa Springstead Cahill. *ADHD in Teens & Young Adults.* All rights reserved.

While we just focused on each sense in a mindful, meditative way, you can also use a simpler version of this strategy. If you recognize that your brain is focusing on worries (or any negative experience) during a day-to-day activity, simply engage one of your senses, such as listening for sounds around you. You can take a deep breath and just listen, or focus on another sense, such as what you might smell, taste, hear, or touch.

MiNDfULnESs ExERcISeS:
Counting to 100

Using our breath as an anchor helps to focus on the "here and now" in day-to-day life, which reduces any worries and thoughts we may find ourselves constantly ruminating about. As you learned in Chapter 1, breathing in specific ways helps to calm the nervous system. These breathing exercises can also help with falling asleep and staying asleep. Here are some additional techniques to add to your toolkit to help with present moment awareness and to calm your body. Try to use the following exercises *before* you react when something upsetting happens, or when you feel internal tension.

Count to 100 Breathing

· If comfortable, close your eyes. If not, focus on an area in front of you with a soft gaze.

· When you are ready, begin counting while you inhale. Fill your lungs completely.

· Pause the count as you breathe out, pushing all the air from your lungs.

· As you inhale and fill your lungs once again, resume your count where you left off.

· Repeat this process until you reach the count of 100.

· You can also start at 100 and count backwards.

How was that for you?

_____

_____

_____

Copyright © 2019, Melissa Springstead Cahill. *ADHD in Teens & Young Adults*. All rights reserved.

MINDFULNESS EXERCISES:
4-7-8 Breathing

The 4-7-8 breathing technique is used to bring relaxation to the body. It shifts energy from the sympathetic (anxious, fight-or-flight) nervous system to the parasympathetic (calming) nervous system. It can also help with lowering blood pressure, reducing heart rate, and letting go of emotional dysregulation. Although this exercise can be done in any position, just make sure to keep your back straight. The breathing ratio in the exercise is important, not the amount of time spent. Given that this breathing strategy can also help with sleep, consider trying it each night before bed.

- Exhale through your mouth (make a *whoosh* sound).

- Close your mouth, and inhale through your nose for a mental count of **FOUR**.

- Hold your breath for a mental count of **SEVEN**.

- Exhale through your mouth making a *whoosh* sound for a mental count of **EIGHT**.

- This is one breath. Repeat the cycle three more times for a total of four breaths. Repeat if needed.

Do you feel any different after doing this breathing exercise?

_____

_____

_____

Copyright © 2019, Melissa Springstead Cahill. *ADHD in Teens & Young Adults*. All rights reserved.

CaSE StUDy — From Teens Like You!

You might be surprised by how powerful a tool the 4-7-8 Breathing exercise can be. A former client of mine, who is now 16 years old, wanted to tell users of this workbook a little bit about what she had struggled with and how the 4-7-8 technique ended up making a difference for her. Here is what she had to say:

"When I first learned about the 4-7-8 breathing technique, I had virtually no prior knowledge of the effects of controlled breathing. I knew that was a thing that people did in yoga, and that's about it. I came in to meet with Melissa for my anxiety, and I was willing to do anything to get it under control. One of the first things she taught me was the 4-7-8 breathing. Breathe in for four counts, hold for seven, breathe out for eight. She told me it was scientifically proven to physically calm you down, and I think that's what sold me on it.

After doing it about four times right there in her office, I was genuinely so surprised about how much it calmed me down in so little time. When I have physical anxiety, like when my heart races and I hear loud white noise coming from my head, 4-7-8 is my first go-to. I usually get that anxiety from scary thoughts or just too much going on in my head, so when I force myself to count my breaths, it takes my mind off of the thoughts that freaked me out in the first place. I think of it as a double-threat in the sense that the breathing chills my body out while the counting guides my mind off of what's happening.

I also tend to have trouble falling asleep, and Melissa says, '4-7-8 until you wake up in the morning!' It works every time. Whether I am about to take a final or I can't fall asleep, I've found the 4-7-8 breathing to be the strategy that gets me through it all."

– A.H., 16

Hopefully, the 4-7-8 technique will be as valuable to you as it was for A.H. It is a tool that you will always have at your disposal, so feel free to use it whenever you think it will provide any kind of benefit to your mental, physical, or emotional health.

BODY SCAN MEDITATION

The body scan meditation was first introduced as a way to help manage pain. It is a form of meditation that focuses on the body, helping to increase attention and decrease both stress and anxiety. It also helps to shift attention away from negative thoughts. Before you begin the exercise:

- Make sure that you are warm and comfortable (take your shoes off if you are comfortable doing so).
- If you are sitting, make sure you are in a comfortable chair with your feet on the floor and your hands resting in your lap.
- If you are lying down, rest your arms comfortably at your side.

Try not to worry about whether or not you are doing everything "right" during the body scan meditation. The purpose of the exercise is to bring awareness to each part of your body—not to judge yourself! When you are ready, begin.

MᵢNDfULₙESₛ ExERₒIₛE:
Body Scan Meditation

Lie down, making yourself comfortable. Allow your eyes to close gently. Take a few moments to get in touch with the movement of your breath and the sensations in your body, especially the sensations of touch or pressure, where your body makes contact with the floor or bed.

On each out-breath, allow yourself to let go, to sink a little deeper into the ground you are laying on.

Remind yourself of the intention of this practice. Its aim is not to feel any different, relaxed, or calm; this may happen or it may not. Instead, the intention of the practice is, as best you can, to bring awareness to any sensations you detect, as you focus your attention on each part of the body in turn.

Now bring your awareness to the physical sensations in the lower abdomen, becoming aware of the changing patterns of sensations in the abdominal wall as you breathe in and as you breathe out.

Having connected with the sensations in the abdomen, bring the focus or spotlight of your awareness down the left leg, into the left foot, and out to the toes of the left foot. Focus on each of the toes of the left foot—in turn, bringing a gentle curiosity to investigate the quality of the sensations you find, perhaps noticing the sense of contact between the toes, a sense of tingling, warmth, or no particular sensation.

When you are ready, on an in-breath, feel or imagine the breath entering your lungs and then passing down into the abdomen, into the left leg, left foot, and out to the toes of the left foot. Then on the out-breath, feel or imagine the breath coming all the way back up, out of your foot, into your leg, up through your abdomen, chest, and out through your nose.

As best you can, continue this for a few breaths, breathing down into your toes and back out from your toes. It may be difficult to get the hang of this—just practice this "breathing into" as best you can, approaching it playfully.

Now when you are ready, on an out-breath, let go of your toes and bring awareness to the sensations on the bottom of your left foot—bringing a gently investigative awareness to the sole of the foot, the instep, the heel, where the heel makes contact with the floor. Experiment with "breathing with" the sensations—being aware of the breath in the background, as in the foreground you explore the sensations of your lower foot.

Now allow the awareness to expand into the rest of your foot—to the ankle, the top of the foot, and right into the bones and joints. Then, taking a slightly deeper breath, directing it down into the whole of your left foot, and as the breath lets go on the out-breath, let go of the left foot completely, allowing the focus of awareness to move into your lower left leg—the calf, shin, knee, and so on in turn.

Copyright © 2019, Melissa Springstead Cahill. *ADHD in Teens & Young Adults*. All rights reserved.

Continue to bring awareness, and a gentle curiosity, to the physical sensations in each part of the rest of your body in turn—to the upper left leg, the right toes, right foot, right leg, pelvic area, back, stomach, chest, fingers, hands, arms, shoulders, neck, head, and face. In each area, as best you can, bring the same detailed level of awareness and gentle curiosity to the bodily sensations present.

As you leave each major area, "breathe into" it on the in-breath, and let go of that region on the out-breath. When you become aware of tension or of other intense sensations in a particular part of the body, you can "breathe into" them—using the in-breath gently to bring awareness right into the sensations and, as best you can, have a sense of their letting go, or releasing, on the out-breath.

The mind will inevitably wander away from the breath and the body from time to time. That is entirely normal. It is what minds do. When you notice it, gently acknowledge it, noticing where the mind has gone off to, and then gently return your attention to the part of the body you intended to focus on.

After you have "scanned" the whole body in this way, spend a few minutes being aware of a sense of the body as a whole and of the breath flowing freely in and out of the body. If you find yourself falling asleep, you might find it helpful to prop up your head with a pillow, open your eyes, or do the practice sitting up rather than lying down. Feel free to experiment while doing this practice at home and try it at different times of day.

From Kabat-Zinn (1990)

How was that for you? What did you notice during the process? Do you feel any different afterward?

_____

_____

_____

Copyright © 2019, Melissa Springstead Cahill. *ADHD in Teens & Young Adults*. All rights reserved.

MULTITASKING

Although it is common for people to think they are multitasking when they attempt to juggle multiple tasks at once, oftentimes they are really only rapidly changing between tasks—not doing them simultaneously. For example, you may be attempting to do your homework while catching up on emails. While you may think that you are multitasking, you are actually shifting rapidly between both tasks as opposed to doing them at the same time—which is ineffective and actually slows you down! The brain is wired so that we are natural **monotaskers**, not multitaskers—it can only do one thing at a time. The more we demand that the brain shift between tasks, the slower we become and the more errors we make. Our desire to multitask explains why many of us have difficulty completing homework in a timely matter. With that in mind, multitasking can have an extremely negative impact on your ability to pay attention, learn, and live a mindful life.

Try experimenting with multitasking by timing yourself and being curious about your performance and how you retain information. See if you notice any difference when you multitask vs. when you monotask. Do you take longer or shorter to complete tasks? Is it easier or more difficult to learn and retain new information? Another aspect to experiment with here is music: People often like listening to music while working. While some background noise can be helpful for people who have a difficult time focusing and paying attention, for others, it does not help. Try experimenting with various types of music and see what works for you. Typically, background music—that is, not something you would normally dance or sing along to—can help drown out outside noises that can sometimes take your attention and focus away from tasks. Reflect below on what you notice while experimenting.

Multitasking

Do you multitask? _____ Yes _____ No

If yes, in what ways to do you find yourself multitasking?

_____

_____

_____

Think about ways that you multitask and consider the following questions:

What is my optimal work environment? How do I actually focus best on my work?

_____

_____

_____

How can I *prevent* myself from multitasking when working in my optimal environment?

_____

_____

_____

Copyright © 2019, Melissa Springstead Cahill. *ADHD in Teens & Young Adults*. All rights reserved.

Reflections on
Monotasking vs. Multitasking

_____

_____

_____

_____

_____

_____

_____

_____

Copyright © 2019, Melissa Springstead Cahill. *ADHD in Teens & Young Adults*. All rights reserved.

SETTING INTENTIONS

It is important to recognize how our behaviors and actions impact what we do and where we go in life. For example, if we make choices that minimize stress and help us to relax and enjoy life, then this increases the chance that we will fulfill our intentions (or goals, as you may have referred to them before learning about intentions vs. goals in Chapter 1). Think about any goals you have previously set in your life. These goals could have been about academics, sports, your social life, family, etc. While thinking about these goals, reflect on the following questions:

- What kind of life do you want to have?
- Do you want adventures?
- Do you want challenges?
- Do you want to be remembered for helping people?
- Do you want to create something or accomplish a specific goal?
- Do you want a quiet life with family, friends, and good food?

Having a vision for our future and setting intentions can make it easier to work a little harder or differently so that we can live the life we see for ourselves. Spend a minute or two (with your eyes closed, if that's most comfortable) and picture your future. This could involve visualizing your life during college, after college, or later in life… whatever comes to you first is perfect. After a minute or two, spend some time visualizing something in the near future that may be causing some stress or worry. For example, if you are in high school, you may be concerned about college and where you will end up. If you are in college, you may be worrying about what comes next. Try to focus on visualizing something that is in the near enough future… picture yourself fulfilling your intention and then visualize how you want that future to be.

On the next page, draw yourself (it can be a stick figure—no need for perfection!). Then, include parts of what you visualized. For example, if you visualized going to college and have an intention of attending in the near future, draw something that symbolizes or is representative of that. Do that for however many things you would like.

TIP: Consider putting your drawing somewhere you can see it every day so that it serves as a gentle reminder of why we use these strategies and exercises to help live happy and fulfilled lives.

Seeing My Future

Copyright © 2019, Melissa Springstead Cahill. *ADHD in Teens & Young Adults.* All rights reserved.

ANCHOR IT!

- ***Mindfulness Meditation Tracking Sheet:*** Try using the breathing strategies and body scan meditation, with at least two days devoted to body scan meditation.

- Practice the ***4-7-8 Breathing Method*** before bed

- ***No Multitasking:***
  - Experiment with monotasking vs. multitasking by timing yourself doing things in different ways.
  - Study in the space (your "optimal working environment") that was described in the multitasking section.

- ***Body Scan Meditation***

Mindfulness Meditation Tracking Sheet

Week of: _____

DAY/DATE	DID YOU PRACTICE?	COMMENTS

Copyright © 2019, Melissa Springstead Cahill. *ADHD in Teens & Young Adults*. All rights reserved.

E: Emotions

LEARN IT!
- Emotions and ADHD

USE IT!
- Mindfulness Exercise: *R.A.I.N.*
- *Loving-Kindness Meditation*
- Other Tips to Manage Emotions

ANCHOR IT!
- *R.A.I.N.*
- *Loving-Kindness Meditation*
- Continue Using Strategies from Previous Weeks
- *Mindfulness Meditation Tracking Sheet*

EMOTIONS AND ADHD

Few people factor in the emotional challenges that are associated with a diagnosis of ADHD. In fact, it is not even a part of the diagnostic criteria. However, people who have ADHD and those who support them know that emotions are a part of the struggle. People with ADHD don't feel a different set of emotions than those without ADHD—rather, they feel both positive and negative emotions more intensely and frequently, and often for longer periods of time. It is often difficult for them to regulate their emotions, which causes them to respond to situations in an emotionally inappropriate way. For example, some adolescents may have a hard time letting go of intense emotions when they are stressed, angry, or experiencing any other negative feeling. They may worry or become annoyed over what others may think are small things. Being sensitive is also a common emotional experience. Adolescents with ADHD frequently say that things "aren't fair" because of their emotional sensitivity. Parents, caregivers, and teachers may find themselves getting frustrated when a person with ADHD "can't seem to let things go."

When we remember that ADHD causes difficulty with executive functioning, it can be easier to have some compassion and understanding in terms of why emotion regulation may be difficult. At the same time, even though ADHD makes it more difficult to regulate our emotions, it does not mean that we can allow each and every one of our emotions to rule our lives and determine how we react the exact moment we feel something. Instead, our goal is to have a foundational understanding of why things are happening and to then make choices that protect against any negative consequences.

However, adolescents with executive functioning difficulties may have trouble seeing the big picture. Instead, they tend to get stuck in whatever they feel in the moment, which leads them to react—vs. respond—to their emotions. As a result, they may avoid difficult tasks out of fear that they will have a negative emotional experience. On the other side, if they do attempt a difficult task, they may give up at any sign of emotional discomfort. They also may feel easily overwhelmed, which can lead them to avoid interacting with others. If any of the above has been true for you in your life, you'll find the tools in this chapter to be very comforting and useful.

When you can stop and say, "This is something that is happening due to my ADHD," and not just because you are "overly emotional," then you can make some changes. You can start to recognize when an emotional response does not feel right. It is only when you become *curious* about your emotions that you can **respond** to a situation rather than **react**. Note the key difference between those two words!

Once you have paused and developed a curiosity about your emotions using the *R.A.I.N.* mnemonic, you can choose how to proceed in the situation using mindfulness strategies, such as breathing techniques and/or guided meditations. The R.A.I.N Tracking Sheet will help to initially guide you through the *R.A.I.N.* exercise. Over time, you may notice that it gets easier and that you no longer need the worksheet. However, in the beginning, using the worksheet is helpful in order to track and learn from your experience. You can use this exercise during (or right before) highly emotional experiences.

MiNDfULnESs ExERcISe:

R.A.I.N.

Using mindfulness strategies can help improve your emotion regulation skills, especially in situations that can initially seem overwhelming. One particular strategy that can help you deal with your emotions more mindfully is to remember the mnemonic **R.A.I.N.** While this technique is best used immediately when you feel a strong negative emotion—or even an intensely strong positive emotion that seems confusing or overwhelming—I recommend that you practice using it right now, in this quiet moment, in order to familiarize yourself with what it is and how it works. The **R.A.I.N.** technique will remind you to:

Recognize what is going on.
- Label with curiosity the feeling that you are experiencing.

Allow and accept the experience to be there, just as it is.
- This does not mean that you have to *like* the feeling.
- Just see if you can accept that it is a feeling you are having now and that it is only temporary.

Investigate with kindness.
- Notice if you are feeling anything in your body like tense muscles, a pit in your stomach, your heart racing, or shallow breathing.
- Notice if you have any thoughts connected to the feeling.

Natural awareness and non-identity.
- Try to not personalize.
- Remember that it is a temporary feeling. It is a wave of emotions, and like all emotions, it will come and go.

Copyright © 2019, Melissa Springstead Cahill. *ADHD in Teens & Young Adults*. All rights reserved.

SaMpLe wORkSHeET:
R.A.I.N. Tracking Sheet

What was the situation?	Recognize	Allow	Investigate	Natural Awareness
	What is going on? What are your thoughts, feelings, and behaviors?	Don't try to block and hide the thoughts, feelings, and behaviors. Allow them to be present without judgment.	Notice what is going on in your body. Note any emotions that are triggered by those physical sensations.	Be aware that the feelings are temporary and that you do not have to attach to them.
EXAMPLE: I had given my parent/caregiver something to proofread, and they returned it with so many corrections that I could hardly see what I had originally written.	I felt anger—hot, burning, face flushing. I thought, "I only asked for your impression, not for you to re-write every word!"	I took notice of my body tension and the slow burn I was feeling, staying with these feelings and sensations without trying to banish them.	Underneath the anger was hurt. I thought I did a good job. Then, I had the recognition that they had spent a lot of time looking at this paper just to help me.	I noticed that the hot anger had dissipated somewhat. Now I could see that with their suggestions, the writing was greatly improved.

Copyright © 2019, Melissa Springstead Cahill. *ADHD in Teens & Young Adults*. All rights reserved.

WORkSHEET:

R.A.I.N. Tracking Sheet

What was the situation?	Recognize	Allow	Investigate	Natural Awareness

Copyright © 2019, Melissa Springstead Cahill. *ADHD in Teens & Young Adults*. All rights reserved.

LOVING-KINDNESS MEDITATION

When adolescents with ADHD have difficulties with emotion regulation, it is not surprising that they often struggle with confidence and self-esteem. For example, you may find that you get frustrated when you realize that you sometimes react in a way that does not feel right, or in a way that differs from your peers. You may also hear messages from other people (parents/caregivers, teachers, siblings, friends, etc.) that you are doing something wrong. Although this can be distressing, there are exercises you can do to help! One technique involves practicing a *Loving-Kindness Meditation*, which helps you to focus and shift your emotional attention more easily. What exactly does that mean? It means that when you experience an intense emotion, you notice that you are able to let go of that emotion sooner than you were previously able to. You may also notice less anxiety, stress, and sadness, as well as an increase in your ability to live a more mindful life.

It is important to remember that change does not happen immediately and that these habits will continue to make your life easier *if you practice them consistently*. If you are not noticing active changes, be patient and understand that change can happen internally. Given this, it is important to also reflect on how the interventions and activities make you feel.

The following is a script for a *Loving-Kindness Meditation*.

Loving–Kindness Meditation Script

This meditation can be done in any position and begins by taking a moment to be aware of any thoughts or feelings you may be experiencing in the current moment. Acknowledge how things are for you *right now*. When you are ready, begin to bring awareness to your body: You are feeling your feet… legs… hips… your lower and upper body… arms… shoulders… neck… head… You are beginning to feel the movement of your breath. The actual sensations of breathing remind you that you are here, alive, and whole…

When you're ready, you might bring to mind the image of a person who you know or have known in your life to be loving and kind to you—someone who easily evokes feelings of warmth and love. It could be a friend, sibling, parent, another family member, a mentor, or a teacher… someone who has been good to you, who helps you feel safe and whole, whose care easily flows from them to you. And, if a person doesn't come to mind from the past or present, imagine someone inspirational who you know will come into your life one day. Imagine sending wishes of well-being to this person. If it feels right, imagine saying to them:

May you be happy, healthy, and whole.

May you have love, warmth, and affection.

May you be protected from harm and free from fear.

May you be alive, engaged, and joyful.

May you experience inner peace and ease.

You may have your own words and wishes for them, so feel free to use words that resonate with you. Picture this person receiving your wishes, and imagine how it might make them feel. Take a few minutes now to feel how it is to wish these things for them, letting yourself have the sense of these wishes of well-being emanating from you to them, connecting you to them. Notice how it feels inside you as you send these wishes of well-being to this person you love or care about.

When you are ready, see if you can imagine this person or figure wishing these very same things for you, knowing that they have your well-being in their heart. Imagine them saying to you:

May you be happy, healthy, and whole.

May you have love, warmth, and affection.

May you be protected from harm and free from fear.

May you be alive, engaged, and joyful.

May you experience inner peace and ease.

Copyright © 2019, Melissa Springstead Cahill. *ADHD in Teens & Young Adults*. All rights reserved.

Letting those feelings wash over you, feeling their unconditional love and caring for you, letting the feelings of love and safety grow in you, know there is nothing you have to do to deserve these feelings and wishes. They are given freely and without condition. See if you can connect to the meaning of these phrases, even if you might not feel all the safety and warmth right now, knowing that is their wish for you. Now, see if you can have these wishes for yourself. Hear yourself say to yourself:

> **May I be happy, healthy, and loved.**
> **May I be safe and protected.**
> **May I be alive and free.**
> **May I experience inner peace and ease.**

You may have loved ones for whom it's also easy to have these wishes, such as a family member or dear friend, or even a loved pet. If it feels right, say to them, in your own way and with your own words:

> **May you be happy and healthy and loved in your life.**
> **May you be safe and protected, and not suffer.**
> **May you be alive and joyful.**
> **May you have inner peace and ease.**

If it feels right, see if there are others in your life to whom you can extend these good wishes—perhaps a friend, a sibling, a parent, a teacher, or a neighbor. Say to them:

> **May you be happy and healthy and loved in your life.**
> **May you be safe and protected, free from harm.**
> **May you be alive and joyful.**
> **And may you have inner peace and ease.**

It might even be possible to expand even further out, to acquaintances—people you know of but with whom you don't yet have a personal relationship. Think about the people you see around town, your neighbors down the block, or even people you don't have strong feelings about, like the salesperson who checks your groceries. Say to these people:

> **May you be happy and healthy and loved.**
> **May you be safe and protected, free from suffering.**
> **May you be alive, engaged, and joyful.**
> **And may you have inner peace and ease.**

And even if the wishes aren't infused with the same warmth and love as they were with a loved one, see if you can extend the wish, without the expectation that it should make you or them

Copyright © 2019, Melissa Springstead Cahill. *ADHD in Teens & Young Adults*. All rights reserved.

feel any particular way. Connect with what these wishes represent, keeping these people in your awareness as you send these good wishes:

The wish for them to be healthy and whole.

The wish for them to feel alive and loved in their lives.

And if you feel strong and secure, and you're comfortable with this, you might try extending these wishes to someone who's difficult for you to deal with right now. Perhaps not necessarily the most difficult person in your life... just someone for whom there's been some sort of frustration or misunderstanding. In doing this, it might help to remember that— just like you—they want to be loved, and just like you, they want peace in their life. Say to yourself:

Just like me, they want to feel happiness and joy.

Just like me, they want peace and ease.

And they want to be loved, and to know that their loved ones are safe and healthy.

And just like me, they are doing the best they can with what inner and outer resources they have.

And if it feels possible to you, imagine silently saying to them:

May you feel peace and ease *(remembering that if this were really true for them, that they would certainly be easier to get along with)*.

May you have love and warmth in your life.

May you be happy, healthy, and whole.

Even if this is difficult, there's value in noticing what it's like to extend the wish, recognizing that you are not condoning their actions, but seeing in them a human being with some of the same needs as you: to be loved, to be safe, and to be at peace.

And, if this is possible, remember the circle that began with yourself and the persons you loved the most—your family and friends—and imagine extending that circle to include all the many people you don't know who may live far away, in other countries or cultures, by saying:

May you be happy and healthy.

May you have peace and ease.

May you have love and warmth in your life.

You could even imagine extending these wishes to include the animals and plants around you, and to all life on our planet and beyond, including ourselves, by saying:

May we all be happy and healthy.

Copyright © 2019, Melissa Springstead Cahill. *ADHD in Teens & Young Adults*. All rights reserved.

May we all be safe and protected.

May we all live together in peace, ease, and happiness.

And now, as this loving-kindness meditation comes to an end, take time to appreciate and feel what's been generated through this practice. Even if there have been difficult parts of this exercise, know that it has the potential to increase your senses of aliveness, connection, and belonging...

When you are ready, let yourself feel your physical presence again: the sensations of your body from your feet, seat, upper torso, neck, and head. Begin to notice the movement of your own breath, bringing life and nourishment to your body as a whole, just as your wishes of good will bring life and nourishment to those around you.

Adapted from Kabat-Zinn (1990)

Copyright © 2019, Melissa Springstead Cahill. *ADHD in Teens & Young Adults.* All rights reserved.

OTHER TIPS TO MANAGE EMOTIONS

One of the hardest things to do is to stop and recognize what our own experience is regarding our emotions. Often, it is easier to blame situations and other people for the feelings we have. The tips described in this book are all ways that help to bring awareness to your experience. By developing an awareness that we can own and change our emotional reactions (or dysregulation), we move closer to living less stressful lives. Below are some additional tips to help manage your emotions:

- **Balance:** Try to make sure that your life is balanced. It should be composed not only of stressful commitments, but of time that you have for yourself.

- **Sleep:** It is easier to stay positive and respond to situations—as opposed to reacting emotionally—when we have had enough sleep. Often, teenagers feel that they need little sleep to function. However, most studies show that teenagers get too little sleep (between 7–7.5 hours each night), when 9–9.5 hours of sleep are actually recommended.

- **Exercise and Nutrition:** When it comes to physical activity, the type of exercise you do is not as important as simply doing something on a consistent basis. For example, you can get into a routine of taking your dog on a daily walk or doing sit-ups and push-ups before homework. Similarly, eating in a way that fuels your body is equally important. Although teenagers often say that they do not have time for breakfast, it is important to eat something to give your brain and body the ability to wake up before being put into stressful situations.

- **Homework and Study Plans:** Having a plan of what to do (and when to do it) helps prevent you from having emotional reactions to last-minute surprises. You have already learned several strategies in this book, such the ***Homework Organizer*** and ***Long-Term Planner***, that can be used to plan ahead. You can also have a to-do list of things that you need to accomplish.

- **Emotions are Temporary:** Remind yourself that no matter how big the emotion you are experiencing, it will fade. Our feelings come and go, so it is helpful to remind ourselves that we will not feel this intensity forever.

- **Take Five:** If you are starting to feel like you may react in a way that you will later regret, then walk away. It could be for as little as five seconds or as long as five minutes—whatever is needed to help your body and mind calm down. It is important to communicate what you are doing if this means walking away from someone mid-conversation.

- **Drop the Mirror:** Try not to take things personally if they don't have to do with you. For example, if you get upset with someone for doing something that you do not agree with, remember that they are allowed to have their own feelings and perspectives. Simply because you have your own opinion about something does not mean that somebody else will (or needs to) have the same opinion.

ANCHOR IT!

- *Mindfulness Meditation Tracking Sheet*

- *R.A.I.N:* When you experience an intense emotion, reference the *R.A.I.N Technique Worksheet* and talk yourself through the experience.

- *Loving-Kindness Meditation*

- Continue using strategies from previous weeks.

Mindfulness Meditation Tracking Sheet

Week of: _____

DAY/DATE	DID YOU PRACTICE?	COMMENTS

Copyright © 2019, Melissa Springstead Cahill. *ADHD in Teens & Young Adults*. All rights reserved.

D: Determination

> **ANCHOR IT!**
> - Reflection and Summary of Previous Weeks
> - Use of Planner/Calendar
> - Importance of Self-Care
>   - *Self-Care Commitment*
>   - *ANCHORED Commitment*

REFLECTION AND SUMMARY OF PREVIOUS WEEKS

- **Chapter 1** was about Attention and Acceptance. Here, you learned what ADHD is and how the workbook is intended to help you across a variety of aspects of your life. You also learned to accept that *you* can use the strategies in this book to help you better address the symptoms of ADHD.

- **Chapter 2** was about Natural Awareness. Here, you learned how being mindful helps with ADHD. You also learned exercises that helped you develop a natural awareness of what happens in your space, mind, and body, as well as with your time.

- **Chapter 3** was about Concentrating on Purpose. This chapter addressed the difficulty you might face when trying to concentrate, and it introduced mindfulness exercises to help improve your ability to focus. You were also introduced to a tool to help you more easily manage homework.

- **Chapter 4** was called Happy Homework, and it made homework the main focus. You learned about the stress behind homework, as well as how to tackle schoolwork in both the short term and long term with a positive mindset.

- **Chapter 5** was titled Open and Organized. It recommended putting yourself in a position where you were open to the idea of integrating new learning strategies, and you learned how effective organization and different study techniques could improve your overall level of happiness.

- **Chapter 6** taught you about the importance of the 3 R's: Recognize, Relax, and Reflect. Here, you learned even more mindfulness exercises to let you recognize and engage your senses in order to relax your body. You also looked at the difference between monotasking and multitasking, and you learned that the human brain is more naturally wired to focus on one thing at one time.

- **Chapter 7** was about your Emotions. You learned that having emotional difficulties is a normal part of dealing with ADHD. You also discovered some ways to manage your feelings, even when they seem intense, scary, or overwhelming.

- **Chapter 8** is our last section of the ANCHORED journey together, and this will be all about **Determination**. That is, the determination to continue to live a mindful life! It is your commitment to remaining curious about finding new ways to help with managing your stress and the symptoms of ADHD that you experience. Determination is all about continuing to walk this path now that you have seen some of the ways that it has benefited you after so much self-discovery and hard work.

If you think about it, determination is yet another form of mindfulness. Thinking back to previous chapters, we have talked about how we only really develop a new skill or trait after a few weeks of practice. Not only is mindfulness needed in order to become comfortable with trying something new, but it is also needed in order to put that "something" into action in the days and weeks that follow. That held true across many of the assignments you have undertaken: from developing an awareness of your daily activities, to learning to be conscious of the feelings in your body during meditation, and even learning how to be mindful of the feelings and experiences of the living things around you. Through these activities, you have learned how to become more attentive, less reactive to situations, more in control of your emotions, more organized, and more able to visualize and plan for your own future.

How have you been able to be so successful? It's because through mindfulness, you have learned (and are continuing to learn) that *you* are powerful and capable. One of the biggest challenges for most people with ADHD is understanding that the diagnosis doesn't define who they are or what they can do. If you started this workbook with a negative self-image, then hopefully many of these activities caused you to reframe how you think about yourself and about your relationship with ADHD. The next few sections will help you to reinforce this aspect of your emotional well-being and keep you moving ahead on this new path.

THE PLANNER/CALENDAR

Many schools have assignments that are completed and submitted electronically, which sometimes makes it feel as if using a calendar or planner is unnecessary. However, it is still important to plan ahead in order to protect against procrastination. In this workbook, you learned how to use the **Homework Organizer** and the **Long-Term Planner** as a way to break down assignments into manageable parts and improve your time management skills. Once you get the hang of using these tools, and your internal clock (estimated time) and external clock (actual time) times are close, you can start transferring your homework assignments onto a regular calendar (or student planner). You may prefer to use an electronic calendar on your phone or computer, or you may want to use a paper calendar—the choice is yours, as long as it helps keep you organized. You should also include social and non-school related items on your calendar. That way, you can combine the use of the **Weekly Schedule**, **Homework Organizer**, and **Long-Term Planner**. At any given moment, you'll have a realistic view of how things look in the near future, as well as in the weeks and months to come. This can be very comforting! You will see how your time is spent, know that some heavy work weeks will pass, and see yourself making progress toward the long-term achievements that once seemed scary!

THE IMPORTANCE OF SELF-CARE

Self-care is any activity that you do on purpose to take care of your overall wellness. It may sound simple, but when we get busy, it is often overlooked. Think about your "plate" in Chapter 1. Did it look like it had enough self-care activities, or were there way more obligations than down time? It's important to make sure that you are constantly making time for things that help you to feel physically and mentally well. When you do, you can boost your confidence and self-esteem.

The following is an exercise to help you develop a commitment to self-care. When we commit and set intentions for ourselves, it is easier to live our lives more mindfully, where we are free of unnecessary stress.

wORkSHeET:
Self-Care Commitment

My reasons for practicing self-care (e.g., to feel less stressed, to remember to have fun):

_____

_____

_____

_____

Ways that I practice self-care:

1. _____

2. _____

3. _____

Support that I need in order to make sure I practice self-care (e.g., maybe you want your parents, a close friend, or another supportive person to remind you to implement self-care practices):

1. _____

2. _____

3. _____

Let's also set a commitment for you to continue with the skills you've learned in this workbook.

Copyright © 2019, Melissa Springstead Cahill. *ADHD in Teens & Young Adults.* All rights reserved.

wORkSHeET:
ANCHORED Commitment

Over the course of completing this workbook, you have learned a lot about how to live a happier, healthier life. Please commend yourself for taking this time to practice the strategies and activities that have been shared with you! Now that you are finished, spend a few minutes making some commitments to help you continue using these tools. For example, you could commit to using the **Homework Organizer**, **Long-Term Planner**, or **Mindfulness Meditation** breathing exercise—or something else! Anything that helps increase your chances of success in continuing to use the skills you have learned.

I commit to doing the following to help me live a more ANCHORED life:

1. _____
2. _____
3. _____
4. _____
5. _____
6. _____
7. _____
8. _____
9. _____
10. _____

I will remember to do these things by (e.g., writing them on a calendar, setting phone alerts, setting reminders):

_____

_____

_____

The people I will reach out to for support are:

_____

_____

_____

Copyright © 2019, Melissa Springstead Cahill. *ADHD in Teens & Young Adults*. All rights reserved.

Guided Meditation Scripts

For your convenience, purchasers can download and print worksheets and handouts from www.pesi.com/ANCHORED

Deep Breathing Meditation

Time: 3 minutes

Sit in a comfortable position with your back away from your chair so you are supporting your spine on your own. Place your feet on the ground. Rest your hands in your lap or on your knees. You may also try placing one hand on your chest and one hand on your lower abdomen so you can feel your breath rise and fall in your body.

- **Notice your body.** Sit comfortably but alert. Your shoulders and hips should be relaxed, and your feet should be touching the floor. Close your eyes.

- **Notice your breath**. Inhale through your nose. Exhale comfortably through the nose, the nose and the mouth, or the mouth only. Notice the rise and fall of your breath in and out of your body. If it helps, you may inhale to a count of four, and exhale to a count of four to eight.

- **Notice what happens.**

  - **Thoughts:** Are you thinking? What are you thinking about? Is your mind wandering? Daydreaming? Making a to-do list? Having memories from something that happened recently or long ago?

  - **Feelings:** What are you feeling? Do you notice any emotions, good or bad?

  - **Sensations:** What do you feel in your body? Is it pleasant? Unpleasant? Neither? Are you feeling achy or tense? Are some areas relaxed?

  - Continue breathing while saying to yourself, "Breathing in, I calm my mind and body. Breathing out, I release what I am holding in my mind and body."

Adapted from Kabat-Zinn (1990)

Copyright © 2019, Melissa Springstead Cahill. *ADHD in Teens & Young Adults*. All rights reserved.

Mindful Eating Exercise

Sitting comfortably in a chair, look at the raisins as if you have never seen them before. Imagine you have arrived from another planet and the raisin is completely new to you. Take the raisin and turn it around. Look at its shape, texture, color, size, temperature, hardness, and softness.

If you find that you are thinking about something else, just notice each thought as it arrives and let it go, bringing your attention back to the raisin. Now, being aware of the movement of your arm, bring the raisin to your nose and smell it. Place it into your mouth, without chewing or swallowing.

Pay attention to all the sensations: texture, taste, shape. When you are ready, take a bite and notice the change. Notice the new texture.

Notice the rest of your mouth. Notice every sensation you can. Now, slowly and consciously chew the raisin. When you are ready, swallow.

Copyright © 2019, Melissa Springstead Cahill. *ADHD in Teens & Young Adults*. All rights reserved.

WORkSHeET:
Test–Taking Guided Meditation

Sit comfortably with your feet on the ground and your eyes closed. You may rest your hands wherever they feel comfortable. Imagine that it is the morning before a test and you have just arrived at school.

As you walk onto campus, you see your friends and classmates. You may even see your teacher. During this time, your mind and body are relaxed. Even though you notice that a few of the students around you are nervous, you feel confident that you did your best to prepare and are ready to take the test. As you get closer to the classroom, you notice your heart starting to beat a little faster. You acknowledge the feeling and remind yourself that you are prepared and ready to take this test.

You are now inside the classroom and seated at your desk. You are prepared and ready to take this test. As the test is passed out, you are calm, focused, and ready to begin. The test has now started.

You are answering each question thoroughly and slowly. You are reading all directions to all problems completely and answering with confidence. Every question you get to is familiar. You have studied and learned the concepts and ideas being asked in the questions. You continue until the test is complete.

You then turn the test in to the teacher and return to your seat. You feel happy that the test is over and accomplished, knowing that your hard work paid off. Enjoy this moment of reflection in knowing you did the best you could.

When you hear the bell, you may open your eyes and return to the room.

Copyright © 2019, Melissa Springstead Cahill. *ADHD in Teens & Young Adults.* All rights reserved.

wORkSHeET:
Body Scan Meditation

Lie down, making yourself comfortable. Allow your eyes to close gently. Take a few moments to get in touch with the movement of your breath and the sensations in your body, especially the sensations of touch or pressure, where your body makes contact with the floor or bed.

On each out-breath, allow yourself to let go, to sink a little deeper into the ground you are laying on.

Remind yourself of the intention of this practice. Its aim is not to feel any different, relaxed, or calm; this may happen or it may not. Instead, the intention of the practice is, as best you can, to bring awareness to any sensations you detect, as you focus your attention on each part of the body in turn.

Now bring your awareness to the physical sensations in the lower abdomen, becoming aware of the changing patterns of sensations in the abdominal wall as you breathe in and as you breathe out.

Having connected with the sensations in the abdomen, bring the focus or spotlight of your awareness down the left leg, into the left foot, and out to the toes of the left foot. Focus on each of the toes of the left foot—in turn bringing a gentle curiosity to investigate the quality of the sensations you find, perhaps noticing the sense of contact between the toes, a sense of tingling, warmth, or no particular sensation.

When you are ready, on an in-breath, feel or imagine the breath entering your lungs and then passing down into the abdomen, into the left leg, left foot, and out to the toes of the left foot. Then on the out-breath, feel or imagine the breath coming all the way back up, out of your foot, into your leg, up through your abdomen, chest, and out through your nose.

As best you can, continue this for a few breaths, breathing down into your toes and back out from your toes. It may be difficult to get the hang of this—just practice this "breathing into" as best you can, approaching it playfully.

Now when you are ready, on an out-breath, let go of your toes and bring awareness to the sensations on the bottom of your left foot—bringing a gently investigative awareness to the sole of the foot, the instep, the heel, where the heel makes contact with the floor. Experiment with "breathing with" the sensations—being aware of the breath in the background, as in the foreground you explore the sensations of your lower foot.

Now allow the awareness to expand into the rest of your foot—to the ankle, the top of the foot, and right into the bones and joints. Then, taking a slightly deeper breath, directing it down into the whole of your left foot, and as the breath lets go on the out-breath, let go of

Copyright © 2019, Melissa Springstead Cahill. *ADHD in Teens & Young Adults.* All rights reserved.

the left foot completely, allowing the focus of awareness to move into your lower left leg—the calf, shin, knee, and so on in turn.

Continue to bring awareness, and a gentle curiosity, to the physical sensations in each part of the rest of your body in turn—to the upper left leg, the right toes, right foot, right leg, pelvic area, back, stomach, chest, fingers, hands, arms, shoulders, neck, head, and face. In each area, as best you can, bring the same detailed level of awareness and gentle curiosity to the bodily sensations present.

As you leave each major area, "breathe into" it on the in-breath, and let go of that region on the out-breath. When you become aware of tension or of other intense sensations in a particular part of the body, you can "breathe into" them—using the in-breath gently to bring awareness right into the sensations and, as best you can, have a sense of their letting go, or releasing, on the out-breath.

The mind will inevitably wander away from the breath and the body from time to time. That is entirely normal. It is what minds do. When you notice it, gently acknowledge it, noticing where the mind has gone off to, and then gently return your attention to the part of the body you intended to focus on.

After you have "scanned" the whole body in this way, spend a few minutes being aware of a sense of the body as a whole and of the breath flowing freely in and out of the body. If you find yourself falling asleep, you might find it helpful to prop up your head with a pillow, open your eyes, or do the practice sitting up rather than lying down. Feel free to experiment while doing this practice at home and try it at different times of day.

From Kabat-Zinn (1990)

Copyright © 2019, Melissa Springstead Cahill. *ADHD in Teens & Young Adults*. All rights reserved.

wORkSHeET:
Loving-Kindness Meditation

This meditation can be done in any position and begins by taking a moment to be aware of any thoughts or feelings you may be experiencing in the current moment. Acknowledge how things are for you *right now*. When you are ready, begin to bring awareness to your body: You are feeling your feet… legs… hips… your lower and upper body… arms… shoulders… neck… head… You are beginning to feel the movement of your breath. The actual sensations of breathing remind you that you are here, alive, and whole…

When you're ready, you might bring to mind the image of a person who you know or have known in your life to be loving and kind to you—someone who easily evokes feelings of warmth and love. It could be a friend, sibling, parent, another family member, a mentor, or a teacher… someone who has been good to you, who helps you feel safe and whole, whose care easily flows from them to you. And, if a person doesn't come to mind from the past or present, imagine someone inspirational who you know will come into your life one day. Imagine sending wishes of well-being to this person, wishing them well. If it feels right, imagine saying to them:

> **May you be happy, healthy, and whole.**
> **May you have love, warmth, and affection.**
> **May you be protected from harm and free from fear.**
> **May you be alive, engaged, and joyful.**
> **May you experience inner peace and ease.**

You may have your own words and wishes for them, so feel free to use words that resonate with you. Picture this person receiving your wishes, and imagine how it might make them feel. Take a few minutes now to feel how it is to wish these things for them, letting yourself have the sense of these wishes of well-being emanating from you to them, connecting you to them. Notice how it feels inside you as you send these wishes of well-being to this person you love or care about.

When you are ready, see if you can imagine this person or figure wishing these very same things for you, knowing that they have your well-being in their heart. Imagine them saying to you:

> **May you be happy, healthy, and whole.**
> **May you have love, warmth, and affection.**
> **May you be protected from harm and free from fear.**
> **May you be alive, engaged, and joyful.**
> **May you experience inner peace and ease.**

Letting those feelings wash over you, feeling their unconditional love and caring for you, letting the feelings of love and safety grow in you, know there is nothing you have to do to

Copyright © 2019, Melissa Springstead Cahill. *ADHD in Teens & Young Adults*. All rights reserved.

deserve these feelings and wishes. They are given freely and without condition. See if you can connect to the meaning of these phrases, even if you might not feel all the safety and warmth right now, knowing that is their wish for you. Now, see if you can have these wishes for yourself. Hear yourself say to yourself:

May I be happy, healthy, and loved.
May I be safe and protected.
May I be alive and free.
May I experience inner peace and ease.

You may have loved ones for whom it's also easy to have these wishes, such as a family member or dear friend, or even a loved pet. If it feels right, say to them, in your own way and with your own words:

May you be happy and healthy and loved in your life.
May you be safe and protected, and not suffer.
May you be alive and joyful.
May you have inner peace and ease.

If it feels right, see if there are others in your life to whom you can extend these good wishes— perhaps a friend, a sibling, a parent, a teacher, or a neighbor. Say to them:

May you be happy and healthy and loved in your life.
May you be safe and protected, free from harm.
May you be alive and joyful.
And may you have inner peace and ease.

It might even be possible to expand even further out, to acquaintances—people you know of but with whom you don't yet have a personal relationship. Think about the people you see around town, your neighbors down the block, or even people you don't have strong feelings about, like the salesperson who checks your groceries. Say to these people:

May you be happy and healthy and loved.
May you be safe and protected, free from suffering.
May you be alive, engaged, and joyful.
And may you have inner peace and ease.

And even if the wishes aren't infused with the same warmth and love as they were with a loved one, see if you can extend the wish, without the expectation that it should make you or them feel any particular way. Connect with what these wishes represent, keeping these people in your awareness as you send these good wishes:

The wish for them to be healthy and whole.
The wish for them to feel alive and loved in their lives.

And if you feel strong and secure, and you're comfortable with this, you might try extending these wishes to someone who's difficult for you to deal with right now. Perhaps not necessarily the most difficult person in your life... just someone for whom there's been

Copyright © 2019, Melissa Springstead Cahill. *ADHD in Teens & Young Adults*. All rights reserved.

some sort of frustration or misunderstanding. In doing this, it might help to remember that—just like you—they want to be loved, and just like you, they want peace in their life. Say to yourself:

> **Just like me, they want to feel happiness and joy.**
> **Just like me, they want peace and ease.**
> **And they want to be loved, and to know that their loved ones are safe and healthy.**
> **And just like me, they are doing the best they can with what inner and outer resources they have.**

And if it feels possible to you, imagine silently saying to them:
> **May you feel peace and ease (remembering that if this were really true for them, that they would certainly be easier to get along with).**
> **May you have love and warmth in your life.**
> **May you be happy, healthy, and whole.**

Even if this is difficult, there's value in noticing what it's like to extend the wish, recognizing that you are not condoning their actions, but seeing in them a human being with some of the same needs as you: to be loved, to be safe, and to be at peace.

And, if this is possible, remember the circle that began with yourself and the persons you loved the most—your family and friends—and remember how you extended that circle to include all the many people you don't know who may live far away, in other countries or cultures, by saying:

> **May you be happy and healthy.**
> **May you have peace and ease.**
> **May you have love and warmth in your life.**

You could even imagine extending these wishes to include the animals and plants around you, and to all life on our planet and beyond, including ourselves, by saying:

> **May we all be happy and healthy.**
> **May we all be safe and protected.**
> **May we all live together in peace, ease, and happiness.**

And now, as this loving-kindness meditation comes to an end, take time to appreciate and feel what's been generated through this practice. Even if there have been difficult parts of this exercise, know that it has the potential to increase your senses of aliveness, connection, and belonging…

When you are ready, let yourself feel your physical presence again: the sensations of your body from your feet, seat, upper torso, neck, and head. Begin to notice the movement of your own breath, bringing life and nourishment to your body as a whole, just as your wishes of good will bring life and nourishment to those around you.

Adapted from Kabat-Zinn (1990)

Copyright © 2019, Melissa Springstead Cahill. *ADHD in Teens & Young Adults*. All rights reserved.

References

For your convenience, purchasers can download and print
worksheets and handouts from www.pesi.com/ANCHORED

Adesman, A. R. (2001). The diagnosis and management of attention-deficit/hyperactivity disorder in pediatric patients. *Journal of Clinical Psychiatry, 3,* 66–77.

American Psychiatric Association. (2013). *Diagnostic and statistical manual of mental disorders* (5th ed.). Arlington, VA: Author.

Babich, A., Burdine, P., Albright, L., & Randol, P. (1976). *CITE Learning Styles Instrument.* Wichita, KS: Murdoch Teachers Center.

Barkley, R. (2012). *Executive functions: What they are, how they work, and why they evolved.* New York, NY: Guilford Press.

Bierdman, J., Newcorn, J., & Sprich, S. (1991). Comorbidity of attention deficit hyperactivity disorder with conduct, depressive, anxiety, and other disorders. *The American Journal of Psychiatry, 148,* 564–577.

Brown, T. E. (2005). *Attention deficit disorder: The unfocused mind in children and adults.* New Haven, CT: Yale University Press Health and Wellness.

Brown, T. E. (2013). *A new understanding of ADHD in children and adults: Executive function impairments.* New York, NY: Routledge.

Faraone, S. V., Sergeant J., Gillberg, C., & Biederman, J. (2003). The worldwide prevalence of ADHD: Is it an American condition? *World Psychiatry, 10,* 104–113.

Harpin, V. A. (2005). The effect of ADHD on the life of an individual, their family, and community from preschool to adult life. *Archives of Disease in Childhood, 90,* 2–7.

Kabat-Zinn, J. (1990). *Full catastrophe living: Using the wisdom of your body and mind to face stress, pain, and illness.* New York, NY: Delacorte Press.

Lange, K., Reichl, S., Tucha, L., & Tucha, O. (2010). The history of attention deficit hyperactivity disorder. *ADHD Attention Deficit and Hyperactivity Disorder, 2,* 241–255.

Leibson, C. L., Katusic, S. K., Barbaresi, W. J., Ransom, J., & O'Brien, P. C. (2001). Use and costs of medical care for children and adolescents with and without attention-deficit/hyperactivity disorder. *JAMA, 285,* 60–66.

MTA Cooperative Group. (1999). A 14-month randomized clinical trial of treatment strategies for attention-deficit/hyperactivity disorder. Multimodal treatment study of children with ADHD. *Archives of General Psychiatry, 56,* 1073–86.

Pastor, P. N., Reuben, C. A., Duran, C. R., & Hawkins, L. D. (2015). *Association between diagnosed ADHD and selected characteristics among children aged 4-17 years: United States, 2011-2013. NCHS data* (Brief No. 201). Hyattsville, MD: National Center for Health Statistics.

Strock, M. (2006). *Attention deficit hyperactivity disorder* [Brochure]. Bethesda, MD: National Institute of Mental Health.

Zylowska, L., Ackerman, D. L., Yang, M. H., Futrell, J. L., Horton, N. L., Hale, T. S., … Smalley, S. L. (2008). Mindfulness meditation training in adults and adolescents with ADHD. *Journal of Attention Disorders, 11,* 737–746.

Made in the USA
Monee, IL
01 November 2021

81170662R00083